MILLER'S
TRADITIONAL
CHRISTMAS

MILLER'S
TRADITIONAL
CHRISTMAS

JUDITH AND MARTIN MILLER

MITCHELL BEAZLEY

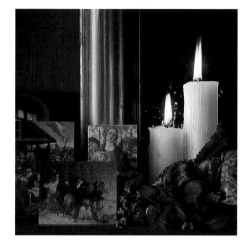

Miller's Traditional Christmas

JUDITH AND MARTIN MILLER

Edited and designed by Mitchell Beazley International Ltd
Michelin House, 81 Fulham Road, London SW3 6RB

Photography **Simon Brown**
Chief Contributor **John Wainwright**
Recipes **Nigel Slater**
Floral Decorations **Paula Pryke**
Stylist **Katrin Cargill**
Assistant Stylist **Rebecca Duke**

Design Director **Jacqui Small**
Managing Editor **Alison Starling**
Art Editor **Trinity Fry**
Production **Sarah Schuman**

The publishers have made every effort to ensure that all instructions given in this book are accurate and safe, but they cannot accept liability for any resulting injury, damage or loss to either person or property whether direct or consequential and howsoever arising. The authors and publishers will be grateful for any information which will assist them in keeping future editions up to date.

Typeset in Baskerville No. 2
by Dorchester Typesetting Group Ltd,
Dorchester, Dorset
Colour reproduction by Mandarin Offset, Singapore
Printed and bound in Great Britain by Butler & Tanner Ltd, Frome, Somerset

CONTENTS

FOREWORD

From my earliest years in Galashiels in the borders of Scotland I have always loved Christmas. I remember it as a time of happiness and excitement, and of a large family gathering that included my parents, my brother Graeme and numerous relations and family friends. The house used to resound with laughter and the days were filled with gifts and the preparation of hot food and drinks. Being Scottish ready hospitality was natural, but especially so over Christmas.

I still feel that original excitement as Christmas approaches; in today's busy world a traditional Christmas seems somehow even more important. It can put some of the meaning and fun back into life, and we can allow ourselves to indulge in a little nostalgia. At the very least, to sit down with the family and make Christmas decorations and presents – much as the Victorians did – or simply to stir the Christmas pudding, helps put into perspective a hectic commercial life throughout the rest of the year.

Our Christmas is spent surrounded by children – my stepchildren Sammy (26), Tanya (21) and Tasha (18), Sammy's daughter Karina (4), and our children Cara (13) and Kirsty (11). My sister-in-law Fiona and her children Lesley (8), Claire (6) and Janis (2) often come to stay, and of course the family wouldn't be complete without my mother Bertha and Martin's father Marc.

Some years we all spend Christmas in our London house, a Victorian artist's studio; others in a 17th-century timbered house in Kent. We also decorate our country-house hotel – Chilston Park – for the festivities. But wherever you have your Christmas, what really matters is the effort you put into making it a success and the pleasure everyone gets out of it.

While Christmas is in many ways a very personal occasion, I hope that much of what we love about it will excite you too. This book is intended as a practical *aide-mémoire* to planning a traditional Christmas, as well as an inspirational treasure trove of festive ideas. Above all it is a reminder that Christmas should be a pleasure, and will be if you prepare well, all muck in and have fun.

A History of Christmas

The Christian festival of Christmas came to British shores in the 4th century AD, when the Roman emperor Constantine, a convert to Christianity, wrote to Augustine, Archbishop of Canterbury, and, shrewdly, instructed him to turn existing pagan festivals into Christian celebrations. Thus, the pagan hordes of Britain did not have to give up their fun in order to take up the new faith of their Roman masters.

The period between the 21st December (the shortest day of the year) and the 1st January had long been a time for festivities. The Vikings held the winter festival of *Juul* (from which our term Yule is derived) in honour of their god Odin on December 21st. Both the Druids and the heathen Romans also had their own celebrations at this time. The Roman Saturnalia, a festival held to honour the god of agriculture and ensure an end to winter and the return of the sun, was a time of charity, when the wealthy presented clothing and money to poorer acquaintances, who in turn gave their rich benefactors garlands, tapers and incense with which to decorate their homes. However, this festival was not strictly a family one; rather, the Roman New Year or *Kalends* celebration was the occasion on which gifts were exchanged between close friends and relatives.

New Year had a place in pagan Britain's festivals too – the 5th of January being known as Wassailing time. Derived from *Wes heill*, which meant to be hale, healthy and free of evil spirits, the festival saw gangs of youths roaming around the fields, banging drums and clashing cymbals to frighten off evil spirits. (This practice was the forerunner of carol singing.) After their vigorous exercise, the young men downed a Wassail cup, which consisted of warm brown ale, sherry, spices, roasted apples and lemons. The practice was vividly commemorated in a traditional rhyme:

"Wisselton, wasselton, who lives there?
We've come to taste your Christmas beer.
Up the kitchen and down the hall,
Holly, ivy and mistletoe;
A peck of apples will serve us all,
Give us some apples and let us go."

With Augustine's encouragement, Christmas gradually became a Christian festival and deep-rooted pagan customs, such as decking the house with greenery, were incorporated into it. The only blow to this successful integration occurred centuries later, when the Puritans denounced the festival as "popish" and passed an Act of Parliament that outlawed it. They declared that the only way to mark the holy day commemorating Christ's birth was by fasting rather than feasting.

Overleaf: *"Christmas comes but once a year!" From the original water-colour drawing by Charles Green R.I., and one of three coloured plates presented with Pears' Christmas Annual of 1896.*
Right: *"The Christmas Tree", by Albert Tayler (1862-1925).*

Left: *"A Merry Christmas" – after the water-colour drawing by Frank Dadd R.I., and one of four plates presented with Pears' Christmas Annual of 1907. Scenes depicting skaters relaxing on the frozen ponds of winter were commonplace in Christmas periodicals and on Christmas cards during the late 19th and early 20th century.*
Right: *"The dinner was served in the great hall" by Cecil Aldin (1908). Christmas dinner was invariably a formal occasion in the manor-houses of England.*
Far right: *"Father Christmas" by Karl Rogers (b.1879).*
Below: *"A Christmas Recital" by Friedrich Ortlieb (1839-1909).*

Much relief was felt at the Restoration of the monarchy in 1660, when this harsh law was repealed. A journal of the time, *Poor Robin's Almanack*, marked the occasion in verse:

"Now thanks to God for Charles' return
Whose absence made old Christmas mourn;
For then we scarcely did it know,
Whether it Christmas were or no
To feast the poor was counted sin,
When treason that great praise did win.
May we ne'er see the like again,
The roguish Rump should o'er us reign."

However, in the meantime many of the old customs and traditions had been lost, although some were rediscovered centuries later – for example, in the 19th century the Victorians brought back to life the Christmas carol (*see* pages 150-155).

The Victorians adored nostalgia and their celebrations often harked back to earlier times. However, they didn't just revive the ancient customs for their old-fashioned Christmases, they also created many new ones that have become a part of our traditional Christmas today. For example, the German Christmas tree (*see* pages 56–69),

the carol "Silent Night" (*Stille Nacht*) and the French cracker (*see* pages 102–115) were all brought to British shores by either entrepreneurial Victorians or immigrants, while other commercially minded individuals introduced the Christmas card and the Christmas pudding (*see* page 134), the latter being derived from the medieval plum pottage or pudding.

Even the 19th-century weather took a hand in forging new traditions: a series of harsh winters during the 1830s

Bethlehem that sheltered the baby Jesus in his manger.

The night before Epiphany is known as Twelfth Night, and in Britain we mark it by taking down the Christmas decorations (it being considered bad luck to leave them up beyond this date). In France, however, Twelfth Night is celebrated in more style. In the true spirit of that nation, the occasion is marked by yet another feast, which finishes with a magnificent cake known as a *Gallete des Rois*, made in honour of the Magi. This confection has a tiny favour (usually a porcelain bean) baked into it, just as the British put a silver charm or sixpence into the Christmas pudding. Whoever finds the bean is dubbed

and 1840s led to the idea of a white Christmas, which continued to be portrayed on festive cards even when snow had once more become the exception, rather than the rule. The idea of a snowy holiday being the perfect Christmas even found its way into fiction, as George Eliot commented in *The Mill on the Floss*:

"Fine old Christmas, with the snowy hair and the ruddy face, had done his duty that year in the noblest fashion, and had set off his rich gifts of warmth and colour with all the heightening contrast of frost and snow."

Thanks in part to the cinema and popular song, we are still dreaming of a white Christmas as we near the end of the 20th century.

Of course, Britain isn't the only country where a traditional Christmas is celebrated, and elsewhere in the world pagan customs have also been incorporated into the Christmas festivities. For example, the early January feasts that livened up the dark nights of winter were adopted into Epiphany, the day when the Three Wise Men – or Magi – bearing their precious gifts of gold, frankincense and myrrh, were said to have followed a star and found their way to the stable in the town of king for the day and is allowed to choose a queen from the assembled company to share his reign. This is certainly a day for the sweet-toothed, for, as well as the Magi's cake, the French festival calls for 13 desserts to mark the journey time of the Magi – 12 days travelling, plus the day of their arrival at Bethlehem.

heating, together with modern methods of building construction, demand an even greater suspension of disbelief.) Our contemporary vision of Santa Claus is in the main derived from a poem, "A Visit from Saint Nicolas", written in 1822 by the American Clement Clark Moore:

Left: *"The Christmas hamper" by Robert Braithwaite Martineau (1826-69). Gift hampers became increasingly popular throughout the 19th century.*
Right: *"The holly-seller's cart", after George Goodwin Kilburne (1839-1924). In Victorian times, town and city dwellers could buy greenery with which to decorate their homes for Christmas from travelling "salesmen" up from the country.*
Far right: *"A large party" by Godefroy Durand (from the* Illustrated London News *of 1881).*
Below right: *"Christmas Visitors Stirring the Pudding" by F.D. Hardy (1826-1911).*
Below left: *Holly for Christmas from "Days of Delight". Victorian (anonymous).*

In Italy, children wait until Epiphany for some of their Christmas gifts, when a good witch named Befana comes down the chimney on a broom and fills their shoes with toys. (There is, however, an unfortunate drawback to this custom: children who have been naughty may find that Befana has left them a heap of ashes rather than a pile of goodies.) In Scandinavia, where there is a similar custom, another woman, Saint Lucy, was said to be the mysterious benefactress.

In the rest of Europe and America gifts are traditionally left by Saint Nicolas or Santa Claus – also known as Father Christmas to the English, *Père Noël* to the French and *Christkindl* to the Germans – who arrives in a sleigh pulled by a team of reindeer, before miraculously entering the house via the chimney. (The advent of central

"... a miniature sleigh and eight tiny reindeer,
With a little old driver, so lively and quick,
I knew in a moment it must be St Nick ..."
He goes on to describe Santa's appearance:
"Down the chimney St Nicolas came with a bound.
He was dressed all in fur from his head to his foot,
And his clothes were all tarnished with ashes and soot;
A bundle of toys he had flung on his back,
And he looked like a pedlar just opening his pack.
His eyes how they twinkled! his dimples how merry!

His cheeks were like roses, his nose like a cherry;
His droll little mouth was drawn up like a bow,
And the beard on his chin was as white as the snow."
And he chronicles Santa's effect on the waiting child:
"He was chubby and plump – a right jolly old elf –
And I laughed when I saw him, in spite of myself."
Today, we imagine the Victorian child living a rather restricted, overly disciplined existence; adults preferring them to be "seen but not heard". At Christmas, however this seems not to have been the case: children stayed up later than usual and joined in the revelries with the adult members of the family. Nothing changes – it's still the case that one of the most exciting aspects of Christmas

for children is being allowed to do things, such as going to Church at midnight or having a sip of sherry, that wouldn't be permitted during the rest of the year.

Of course, Christmas wasn't only a time of excitement for children. Although today we sometimes complain about the over-commercialization of the festival, to the Victorian shopping for cards, gifts, food and drink in shops and stores bustling with seasonal activity and atmosphere was as much part of the pleasure and tradition of Christmas as sitting down with all the family to write greetings cards, making and putting up home-made decorations and preparing the feast.

CARDS

In the 18th century, at the end of their winter term, pupils would be set writing exercises to work on. Known as "Christmas pieces", these were produced on high-quality paper with engraved borders and were presented to parents to show them how well their children had progressed at school during the year. The practice continued into the 19th century and the "pieces" gradually became more elaborate and decorative. For example, by about 1820 the engraved borders were often embellished with colour.

These simple offerings were the forerunners of the Victorian Christmas card, which appeared in 1843. However, the first card was no child's exercise, although it came into being because its originator, like many a schoolboy with his "Christmas piece", was late delivering his duty letters. The tardy character was Sir Henry Cole, a civil servant and founder of what is now the Victoria and Albert Museum, who solved his personal dilemma by asking a friend, Sir John Callcot Horsley, R.A., to design a special card that he could send instead.

Printed and then hand-coloured, the card portrayed a family group quaffing a seasonal glass of wine, flanked on either side by allegorical vignettes depicting acts of charity and framed by a rustic bower of gnarled wood and ivy. The finishing touch was a note of greeting: "A Merry Christmas and a Happy New Year to you." While some of the subject matter offended the temperate classes, the card caused such a stir that in 1846 a thousand of them were printed and sold for a shilling each (a substantial sum in those days). Sadly, few have survived the intervening years.

Victorian entrepreneurs were quick to capitalize on the public interest in Sir Henry's card. In 1844 a Mr Dobson produced one depicting the "Spirit of Christmas", which sold in the thousands, while an etching designed by W.M. Egley in 1848 was the first card to depict holly, together with mistletoe, cherubs and, from Pantomime, a harlequin and columbine.

However, the Christmas card boom that followed might never have happened if the Penny Post had not been introduced by Sir Rowland Hill in 1840. Prior to that, most of the poorer sections of the population disliked receiving mail because it was the recipient, not the sender who had to pay the postman on delivery, and the cost was often quite steep.

By the 1860s English printers had become wise to the business potential of the Christmas card and started to manufacture them in quantity – mass production making them affordable to the less well off. The earliest mass-market cards were sold in sheets of twelve; each one being the size of a visiting card. The buyer cut them out and either delivered them by hand, as they would a

Right: Reproduction late Victorian and early 20th-century Christmas cards, displayed with candles, ribbons and dried flowers on the mantelshelf in The Library at Chilston, our hotel in Kent.

standard visiting card, or enclosed them with a traditional Christmas letter. Given the simplicity of the designs, many adults and children took to customizing their cards with ribbons, paper lace, fabrics or pressed flowers; packets of paper trimmings being available from stationers' shops specifically for this purpose.

In 1880, a greater variety of cards became available over the counter as manufacturers Raphael and Tuck began to produce them in all shapes and sizes and in a range of prices to suit all pockets. Cards cut out to the shape of artist's palettes and half-crescent moons were

satin, silk, plush and brocade, lace and embroidery often providing a decorative twist. Moreover, the Victorian stationer's customer could choose from a dazzling array of designs. Among the most popular were landscapes, especially romantic winter scenes of snow-encumbered stage coaches and cosy cottages. Secular subjects proved just as acceptable as religious ones, and comic cartoon cards were also much in demand.

The period from 1880 to 1890 has been described as the heyday of the Victorian Christmas card, with more than 200,000 different designs on the market by 1895. By

Late 19th- and early 20th-century cards. The one on the left is a "mechanical". The flowers and foliage can be made to "pop-up" by pulling the paper tab on top.

particularly popular, as were novelty "pop-up" and jewelled and embossed cards and imitation cheques and railway tickets. At the same time cards began to appear in ever greater numbers from private presses, their subject matter, influenced for example by the Aesthetic and Arts and Crafts Movements, appealing to the more design-conscious of the day.

Just as the shapes of Christmas cards become more elaborate as manufacturers vied with each other to attract the public with the latest novelty, so the materials that cards were made of became more exotic, with

then the practice of sending Christmas cards through the mail had become so popular that the Post Office often had difficulty coping with the seasonal deliveries. Regular mail was also adversely affected, to the extent that a number of irate citizens wrote to *The Times* complaining that this "frivolous" festive custom had got out of hand.

With competition intense, many card manufacturers vied with each other to produce the finest picture or verse. In fact one company went so far as to offer £10,000 for the best design and, in 1884, commissioned a collection of drawings for Christmas cards from some of the

finest artists of the day, including Walter Crane and Kate Greenaway. Writers benefitted too: the poet Tennyson was said to have been offered a thousand guineas for a short verse, and George Eliot and Christina Rossetti are also known to have tried their hand at penning lines for Christmas cards.

Because relatively few have survived, original examples of Victorian Christmas cards are now highly collectable (and fairly expensive). However, excellent reproductions of Victorian cards are available today from specialist suppliers (for a list of names and addresses, *see* The Directory on pages 157–158).

As an alternative to buying commercially available cards you can of course design and make your own using a variety of traditional techniques – a personal touch that is always appreciated by the recipient. On the following pages we show you how to stencil a simple Christmas motif on to plain or coloured paper – a technique that is particularly suitable, after a little parental guidance, for younger members of the family. For slightly older children we have included illustrations and instructions showing how to embellish blank cards with Christmas images made from paper filigree – a technique, known as Quilling, that originated in the monasteries and nunneries of 15th-century Europe, was a popular pastime among young ladies in England during the 18th century and was adapted by the Victorians during the 19th century for Christmas decoration. Finally, we show you how to make a modern version of the "pop-up" cards that first appeared in the latter half of the 19th century.

Of course, the pleasure of Christmas cards is as much in the receiving as the sending. Whether we are spending the holiday at our home in Kent or town-house in London, cards are always a prominent feature of our Christmas decorations. Pinned to ribbons and hung from picture rails, grouped on side-tables, windowsills or mantelshelfs, or simply "Blu-Tacked" to the walls, they are a confirmation that Christmas is, above all, a time for wishing our family, friends and fellow man well for the season and the coming year.

Above and below: *Displays of cards on the sill and card table in the Chinoiserie Room at Eldon Lodge.*

Left: *As an alternative to simply propping up or standing Christmas cards on a flat surface they can be pinned to gold or silver wire-edged silk or polyester ribbon embellished with decorative bows, and hung from the walls or the overmantel, as here above the downstairs sitting room fireplace at Eldon Lodge.*

1

2

3

STENCIL CHRISTMAS CARD

Stencilling is a quick and easy way for young children to make their own Christmas cards. While the simplest approach is to buy a stencil kit from a DIY or craft shop, Kirsty (aged 10) prefers to design her own – although Martin or I always insist on helping her cut out the stencil with a craft knife.

MATERIALS

Sheet of oiled stencil card; HB pencil; masking tape; scissors; craft knife; cutting board (or thick card); coloured cartridge paper; 3 saucers; small sponge; green, red, black and white artist's acrylics; water.

1 Start by drawing freehand with an HB pencil the outlines of the holly leaves and berries directly onto the oiled card. Next, carefully cut them out with a craft knife.

(To minimize the risk of the blade slipping off line when cutting around a curve, turn the card round the blade rather than the blade round the card.) Then, using strips of masking tape, secure the stencil in position on a piece of coloured cartridge paper cut out to the required size of the card.

2 Squeeze a little green and red artist's acrylic colour into two saucers and pour some water into a third one. Having lightly moistened the sponge with the water, dip it into the green paint. Don't overload the sponge and remove excess paint by dabbing it off onto a spare piece of paper. Then lightly dab the sponge over the holly leaf cut-outs, recharging it with more paint if necessary. You can give the stencil an extra dimension by adding a touch of black paint to the green to create shadows on parts of the leaves, or white paint to produce highlights.

3 To stencil the berries onto the card, simply repeat step 2 using the red artist's colour. However, make sure you wash out your sponge thoroughly in water, and squeeze it nearly dry, before proceeding.

4 Once the paint has dried (this will take up to half an hour), remove the stencil to reveal the finished motif.

1   2   3

QUILLWORK CHRISTMAS CARD

Quilling, or the art of paper curling, is an ancient craft. In Europe it dates back to the 15th century, when monks and nuns used the tips of birds' feathers (quills) to roll thin strips of paper into various shaped scrolls, which were then applied to religious pictures and manuscripts as a form of decoration. A fashionable pastime among young ladies during the 18th century, quilling became a popular method of embellishing Christmas cards during the latter half of the 19th century and is taught in many schools today.

MATERIALS

Quilling kit, which contains: thin coloured strips of quilling paper; quilling tool; coloured art paper; white glue (PVA); applicator sticks. You will also need: HB pencil; compass (or small pot); gold spray paint.

1 Cut a 7½cm/3in strip of green paper and insert one end into the slot in the quilling tool. Turn the tool round, rolling the paper into a tight coil. Remove and allow the paper to slacken off slightly. Apply a spot of glue with the applicator to the free end, and close to form a loose circle. After the glue has dried, pinch together one

side of the circle to form a slightly elongated teardrop shape.

2 Cut a card from the art paper, spray it with gold paint and lightly mark out a circle with a 6½cm/2½in circumference using the base of a pot (or a compass).

3 Using small spots of glue, stick the green teardrop shapes at various angles around the circle. (Cara used 40 shapes.) Next make eight red rosettes, using the same basic technique described in step 1. However, this time keep the circles as tight as possible while applying the glue and don't pinch them out of shape. Then glue them on top of the teardrops.

4 To make a red bow: form a double loop from a single strand of paper. Lightly curl the ends of a second strand in the quilling tool and drape it over and between the loops. Glue a single red rosette over the join and finally glue the bow to the top of the wreath.

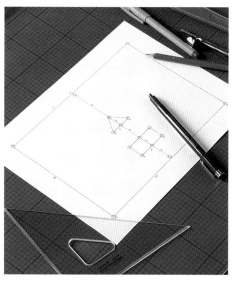

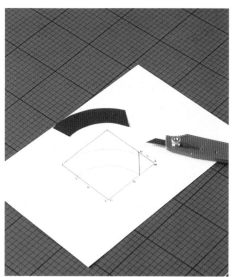

"POP-UP" CHRISTMAS CARD

Mechanical Christmas cards first appeared during the late 19th century. Most worked by pulling a cord or tab, lifting a flap or simply opening by hand, to reveal a three-dimensional "pop-up" scene. They sold in large numbers to a Victorian public keen to find novel ways of sending festive greetings, and have remained popular ever since. Reproduction Victorian cards, like those shown

opposite, can be bought from specialist outlets (*see* The Directory). However, it's more fun, and cheaper, to make one yourself, such as our "pop-up" snowman.

MATERIALS

Cutting board (or thick card); metal ruler; craft knife; scissors; blunt knife; set-square; compass; HB pencil; black, red and green felt-tip pens; wax crayons; stiff blue, white and black art paper; tartan wrapping paper; petroleum-based glue (e.g. Bostick clear).

1 Mark out the template. Black lines mark where you will cut the card. Red dotted lines mark where you will score the front. Green dotted lines mark where you will score the back.

2 Place the template on blue art paper and press the point of a compass through all junctions marked O. Remove the template and join up the holes by cutting and scoring the lines as indicated in step 1. When cutting, use a craft knife against a metal ruler. When scoring, press very

lightly with a blunt knife to compress the paper so it will fold easily – don't cut it.

3 Gently fold the card in half, pushing the triangle and rectangle forward. Then use a compass, pencil and craft knife to mark and cut out the snowballs and head and body of the snowman on a sheet of white art paper. The radius of the snowballs is 1cm/½in, while the snowman's body is 4cm/1⅝in and the head 2cm/¾in.

4 Make the arc for the snowballs by drawing a 6cm by 6cm/2⅜in by 2⅜in square on blue art paper (for clarity, this is shown on white paper). Set the compass to 6cm/2⅜in, place the point on the lower left-hand corner of the square and draw an arc across the top of the square. Set the compass to 4cm/1⅝in and repeat. Having marked the point 2cm/¾in up on the right-hand side of the square, draw a line across (as shown), and cut out the arc.

5 Decorate the card, arc and snowman with wax crayons, and cut out a hat from black art paper and a scarf from tartan wrapping paper. Glue the snowballs to the arc, and the pointed end of the arc to the right side of the triangle (X). Check the arc moves freely when the card is opened and closed.

6 Glue the scarf and hat onto the snowman, tilting the latter slightly to the right so it doesn't catch on the snowballs. Finally, align the snowman against the left side of the rectangle (X) and glue in position, checking it moves freely and trimming the scarf if it sticks out of the side.

HOUSE DECORATION

The custom of decorating homes with evergreens for winter festivals predates the Christian Christmas. The Romans were known to have garnished their villas with holly for the New Year celebrations, as a symbol of the renewal of life, while for the Anglo-Saxons mistletoe had Druidic associations and was thought to protect homes against witchcraft as well as ensuring the fertility of the occupants. Perhaps the folk memory of the second of these beliefs is at the root of the traditional kiss beneath the mistletoe.

Before the introduction of the Christmas tree (*see* pages 56–69), a mistletoe arrangement was often the centrepiece of the festive house. These kissing boughs were made from hoops of wood or metal, and were decorated with mistletoe and apples. Even the prim and proper Victorians indulged in this custom; Charles Dickens chronicled it thus in *The Pickwick Papers*:

"From the centre of the ceiling of this kitchen, old Wardle had just suspended with his own hands a huge branch of mistletoe, and this same branch of mistletoe instantaneously gave rise to a scene of general and most delightful struggling and confusion; in the midst of which Mr. Pickwick with a gallantry which would have done honour to a descendant of Lady Trollimglower herself, took the old lady by the hand, led her to the mystic branch, and saluted her in all courtesy and decorum."

The Victorians decked their homes with a mass of greenery and everlasting flowers, as well as colourful paper trimmings. No Christmas was thought to be complete without mistletoe, holly and ivy. Enterprising street sellers would tour the cities and towns, their carts piled high with holly for sale. The plant material was used in abundance: front doors were hung with welcoming wreaths, banisters twined with thick leafy ropes and garlands and mantels heaped with glistening evergreen boughs, while on the walls gilt frames glinted through swathes of holly and ivy.

As a typical 17th-century timbered Kentish house, our Sissinghurst home is well suited to this traditional, predominantly natural style of decoration. We take the theme through the whole house, starting with a well-berried holly wreath on the front door to welcome visitors. Once inside, our guests move past the ropes and garlands of ivy twined around the banisters in the hall to the living rooms, where a cornucopia of natural decorations is on show: from a candle-lit tree standing next to a blazing log fire to a garland of nuts hanging from the mantelpiece in the inglenook (although I make sure that the holly is out of reach of small children and pets as the berries are poisonous). For our country Christmases, we

Right: A wreath of blue pine, ivy trails, variegated holly and holly berries welcome visitors at the entrance to our home at Sissinghurst. Just inside the door a display of "Baccarolla" and "Bahamas" roses, Singapore orchids, mimosa, spurge, variegated holly and ivy trails stands beneath a garland of variegated holly along the top of the wall.

gather whatever greenery is available from the garden – there is usually a plentiful supply of bay, mistletoe and holly – and bring armfuls into the house; if we intend to spend the festive season in our London home we fill the boot and interior of the car with as much as it will take, even if it does make for a rather uncomfortable journey for anyone sitting in the back. Once home to a Victorian artist and filled with eccentric architectural detail, Eldon Lodge, our London house, allows us to indulge in more exuberant

can exercise their artistic abilities. The children, for example, join in by adding a festive air to their own bedrooms, making, among numerous other things, paper chains as well as decorating their own Christmas tree (*see* pages 52–53 and 64–65 respectively).

As far as decoration is concerned, Eldon Lodge encourages the dramatic – rather like the mood before a fancy dress party, there is an excitement to arranging the frills and furbelows, together with an eager anticipation of the

Left: *We decorated the wicker tree on the marquetry table at the foot of the stairs at Sissinghurst with a selection of reproduction Victorian Christmas cards, festive sheet music and small toys and trinkets such as paper drums and rocking horses. (Wicker trees are available from selected florists and garden centres – see* The Directory, *pages 157–158.)*

We also draped ivy trails from the top of the gilt mirror behind and hung a simple garland of pine cones and ivy trails from the oak beams and around the top of the walls.

Natural decorations such as these, made from gleanings from the forests, fields and gardens (and the florist and local garden centre) are far more in keeping with the style and atmosphere of a traditional country interior than gilt and glitter – the latter being better suited to homes in the city and town.

Left: *To decorate the newel post of the banisters in the hall at Sissinghurst we made up a garland consisting of dried eucalyptus, dried lotus flower heads, tiny cream-coloured roses, small pine cones and bunches of cinnamon sticks tied with braid and ribbon.*

To assemble the garland we employed the same basic wiring techniques used to make make a nut garland (see pages 40–41), a Christmas wreath (see pages 38–39) and a fruit cone (see pages 110–111).

The garland was given an additional festive touch by wiring in miniature Christmas crackers and looping in lengths of "Silent Night" ribbon. (Reproduction Victorian ribbons printed with the words and music to traditional Christmas songs and carols are available from specialist suppliers, see The Directory, *pages 157–158.)*

decorative schemes. I begin by making an elaborate wreath for the front door (*see* pages 38–39) and then I find a large urn or pot and put together an appropriately scaled flower arrangement to stand in the hallway. Meanwhile, Martin relishes the task of constructing still-life *tableaux* that incorporate greenery, fruit, nuts and antiques, and rises to the not inconsiderable challenge of decorating the monumental oak fireplace that dominates the Victorian Gothic studio room (*see* pages 48–51).

Christmas is, of course, a time when the whole family

entertainment and delights that are about to begin.

Parties are also an important part of Christmas at Chilston Park, our country house hotel, and it is never forgotten when we sit down at the end of November to make our decorative plans. In the weeks before Christmas, when the celebrations are at their height, we deck out all the reception and dining rooms with greenery and traditional decorations, both natural and man-made, so as to put all our guests in the Christmas spirit from the moment that they arrive.

The practice of decorating the house with evergreens at Christmas can be traced back to the Roman festival of Saturnalia, the Feast of the Birth of the Unconquered Sun and the Norsemen's celebration of the Feast of the Winter Solstice (Yuletide).

Bringing greenery into the house was supposed to make a retreat for the wood gods and goddesses from the seasonal storms and cold of winter – a pagan belief that accounts for the fact that at one time evergreens were discouraged in Christian households. However, their use has been almost universal for hundreds of years now.

One of the most attractive ways of displaying greenery in the house at Christmas is to make up a garland and embellish it with fruit, flowers and

Top: *A Victorian Christmas card (c.1880).*
Bottom: *"With all my heart I wish you a Merry Christmas".*

decorative ribbons. For example, the garland decorating the banisters at Eldon Lodge (*see* opposite) was made by first binding sprigs of bay leaves and rosemary to heavy-duty string with lengths of florist's reel wire.

Having established the basic "chain", small groups of pimentos were wired in, together with small bundles of cinnamon sticks, tied with fine gold braid, and pine cones – the latter positioned throughout in groups of three.

Poppy flower heads, sprayed gold, and dried roseheads were also wired in to the garland, before the finished article was attached to the banisters by looping wire-edged tartan ribbon through the back of tartan bows made from the same fabric.

CHRISTMAS WREATH

Every year we make a Christmas wreath out of gleanings from the woods, fields and gardens and hang it as a festive welcome on the door of our London house. Easy to make, it always seems to bring a breath of the country to the city.

MATERIALS

Sphagnum moss wreath (or wire frame, blue reel wire and moss to make your own); florist's stub wire; variegated holly; eucalyptus; ivy; blue spruce; skimmia; southern beech; rosemary; pine cones; chilli peppers; baby turnips; Spanish onions; asparagus; root ginger; artichokes; pimentos; holly; snake grass; dried mushrooms; paper, metallic and wire-edged taffeta ribbon.

1 Bind damp sphagnum moss around the frame using blue reel wire.
2 Cut sprigs of holly, ivy and eucalyptus and make into bunches. Twist stub wire around the stems and push into the moss. Attach sprays of blue spruce, skimmia, southern beech and rosemary with wires bent into "hairpins" and pressed over the stems diagonally into the moss.

3 Wire the pine cones (*see* page 40), and the onions, root ginger and baby turnips (*see* page 110), and attach. Bunch the asparagus and snake grass. Bind with wire, twisting the ends into a prong, and cover with ribbon before attaching.
4 Take a length of taffeta ribbon and make three loops, scrunching together where they cross. Bind with wire, twisting the ends together at the back into a prong, and cover with more ribbon, leaving the ends hanging. Attach to the wreath. Make a ribbon loop, wire the ends together and attach opposite the bow.

NUT GARLAND

Making a nut garland to hang from the mantelpiece is great fun, but quite time-consuming – so it's a project for all the family during the run-up to Christmas. Wire in the nuts and seedheads to the moss tubes as you wish or, as we did here, attach them in clearly identifiable groups to the middle section and, for contrast, at random to the outer ones.

1

2

Chicken wire; sphagnum moss; light- and medium-gauge florist's stub wire; glue; pine cones; brazil nuts; hazelnuts; walnuts; almonds; love-in-a-mist seedheads.

1 Make three curved, moss-filled tubes by enclosing sphagnum moss in chicken wire.

2 Loop stub wire around the base of each pine cone, twist and push into the moss.

3 Pierce the bottoms of hazelnuts with wire and secure with a blob of glue. Loop one end of a wire, press flat onto the underside of brazils and secure with glue.

4 Wire walnuts and almonds by piercing the bottoms and securing with glue, and twist light-gauge wire around the stems of love-in-a-mist seedheads.

3

4

41

The inglenook at Sissinghurst (see left) is an ideal place to display the home-made nut garland illustrated on the previous page. To show it off at its best, we draped it across the front of the 17th-century carved oak fireplace – the overmantel of which was embellished with a variety of natural decorations – and lit a warming log fire in the grate below. Continuing the theme, the Christmas tree to the left of the fire was also dressed with natural decorations (details of which are shown and described on pages 66–67).

In one of the niches of the overmantel (top left) a plain terracotta pot holds a candle in a bed of pine cones and assorted nuts, while other candles nestle among the greenery. Candles look particularly effective presented in pairs, but you should note that when grouped in this way the additional heat generated makes them burn faster than usual. In another niche (bottom left) a terracotta pot has been topped with a nut cone (for method of construction, see pages 110–111). A wreath made from nuts, ferns, greenery and tied cinnamon sticks hangs in the centre of the overmantel (top right), while tassels of pine cones strung on rope and decorated with holly sprigs hang from the ends of the mantelshelf (bottom right).

Above: *Garlands and swags of blue pine, variegated holly, yew, sprigs of "Red Kangaroo" paws, miniature antique terracotta flowerpots filled with sphagnum moss, and tartan bows hang from the fire surround in* The Red Sitting Room at Sissinghurst. *Illuminated by the candelabrum, a collection of original and reproduction Victorian "mechanical" cards is displayed on the mantelshelf.*

Top left: *Victorian-style Christmas stockings made from green velvet and gold brocade trim hang from a garland on the red room overmantel.* Above left: *Antique terracotta pots and sphagnum moss, blue pine,*

"Red Kangaroo paws" and tartan bows wired into the garland below. Top right and above right: *Candles and a garland of antique ribbon, pine cones and ivy on the mantelshelf in The Library at Chilston.*

DECORATING THE FIREPLACE AT ELDON LODGE

The fireplace has always provided a focal point for winter festivals, both pagan and Christian. On a practical level, fire was a source of much-needed heat and light in the colder climate of the northern hemisphere. However, the fact that it became such a powerful symbol of celebration explains why, despite the advent of modern central-heating, it remains at the heart of a traditional Christmas today.

Draped in greenery, piled high with fruit and nuts and appropriately festive artefacts, illuminated with candles and with a sweetly scented log fire crackling in the grate, the fireplace in The Studio at Eldon Lodge is a celebration of the winter festivals of all our ancestors.

The fire-surround was constructed according to the instructions of the original Victorian artist-owner of the house from an eclectic collection of 17th–19th-century carved and decorated wooden panelling. And it has a particular relevance to Christmas as the flanking panels above the overmantel (*see* previous page) both depict a Madonna and Child.

When deciding on the decorations, Martin felt they should to some extent reflect the original artistic purpose of the room. The finished article (*see* opposite, top left) certainly looks like it could have featured as a still-life in a Pre-Raphaelite painting. However, his main intention was to create an effect that was as much a celebration of Nature as of Man's Art.

The ivy, which Martin wound generously around the pillars, trailed over the overmantel and allowed to spill down over the piles of logs (*see* above left), plays a key part in this – it looks as if it was growing there naturally.

Illumination was provided by candles of various sizes. Some were grouped on the mantelshelf around a central candle on an 18th-century mahogany candlestand. Flanking candles were secured in French Empire-style brass candlesticks (*see* above centre). All the candles have a high beeswax content, and so when lit add their honeyed scent to the sweet smell of burning applewood in the grate.

Martin then added various artefacts – each one representing various elements of the Christmas celebrations, grouping them in a series of artist's 'still-lives'. *Opposite top right:* a Victorian brass-mounted, engraved glass claret jug; a 17th-century ivory-mounted hourglass on an 18th-century wooden candlestand; a 19th-century treen goblet; a Victorian treen nutcracker; a 19th-century brass carriage clock; a Victorian papier-mâché casket, inlaid with tortoiseshell and mother-of-pearl; and some Roman pottery beads. *Opposite bottom right*: A late 19th-century Vienna plate; a Victorian soapstone sleeping child; and some 18th- and 19th-century leather-bound books. *Opposite bottom left:* An 18th-century lime-wood figure; a 19th-century book of common prayer; an 18th-century airtwist-stemmed English drinking glass; and an 18th-century ale glass.

To complete the theme, Martin placed an abundance of oranges, kumquats, grapes and apples, nuts and pine cones and mistletoe – the fruits of nature – in and around the man-made artefacts.

PAPERCHAIN

Instead of buying paperchains to decorate the room for their children's Christmas tea party, Cara and Kirsty (shown here) have great fun making them up from sheets of colourful wrapping paper. Rather like daisy chains, once you've got the knack they're very simple to do and, unlike daisy chains, they can be stored away and re-used the following year.

MATERIALS

Sheets of thick wrapping paper in various colours and patterns; sheets of red crêpe paper; clear glue; metal ruler; pencil; scissors (or a craft knife); drawing pins (or Blu-Tack or Sellotape).

1 Stick two sheets of wrapping paper, each a different colour and pattern, back to back and allow the glue to dry. Next, using a ruler and pencil, divide the double sheet into 5cm/2in strips and then cut them out accurately with scissors or a craft knife and metal ruler. (If you intend to make a very long chain, you can increase the width of the strips by anything up to about 2½cm/1in.)

2 To make the first link in the chain, simply overlap the two ends of a strip and glue them together, holding firmly in position until dry. You can adjust the size of the link by either trimming one end before glueing, or by increasing the overlap, but make sure all the links in the chain are the same size.

To make the next link, thread a strip through the first link so that the pattern on the outside is the same as the pattern on the inside of the first link. Overlap and glue as before, and then repeat this process until the chain is the required length.

3 Make the bows by first twisting a sheet of crêpe paper into a cord and cutting it into 6½cm/2½in lengths. Next, wrap a short length – approximately 2½cm/1in –

Right: *Cara and Kirsty play host to their young friends and niece Karina at the children's tea party at Eldon Lodge.*

of the cord around the middle of the first piece and glue in position. Having gently fanned out the ends of the bows, simply glue them onto the outside of alternate links in the chain.

Finally, use drawing pins, Blu-Tack or Sellotape to secure the ends of the chain (or chains) in position (as *opposite*).

THE TREE

Originally, Christmas trees were a German tradition, dating back as far as the 15th century. Although Queen Charlotte, wife of George III, set one up at Windsor Castle in 1789, it was not until Queen Victoria's consort, Prince Albert, reintroduced the custom in the 1840s – importing fir trees from his native Coburg – that the British public took up the fashion. In the 1848 edition of the *Illustrated London News* the Royal Family was portrayed at Windsor, gathered around their tree. Thereafter, the Christmas tree became an essential part of the seasonal celebrations in Britain, from where the custom soon spread to America.

The earliest tree decorations were hand-made and consisted of strings of popcorn, apples, nuts, bonbons and preserved fruits. Wax tapers or gelatine candlecups were fixed to the branches and lit on Christmas Eve, when all the family were assembled. This was also the time that the multitude of small gifts hung from the tree – toys and trinkets intended for the children – were distributed.

The candles were lit when the tree was attended, and then only for a short time because of the obvious risk of fire. Martin, the children and I follow this custom today; preferring the soft glow and pleasant smell of beeswax candles to the harsher, albeit pretty light given off by the odourless electric alternative.

You may wonder why such a potentially unsafe form of decoration was adopted. While the magical appearance of a candle-lit tree was part of the attraction, it is also said that Martin Luther, professor of theology at the Saxon University of Wittenberg, *c.* 1517, and instigator of the Reformation in Europe, originated the practice to remind young children of the starlit heavens from which Jesus, the Son of God, descended to earth.

If the idea of decorating your Christmas tree with candles worries you, be reassured that electric lights are not as modern as you may think, and so not completely out of step with a traditional tree. The first electric lights were said to have belonged to a New York associate of Thomas Edison, one Edward Johnson, who illuminated his tree with them in 1882. Just ten years later General Electric put the idea into commercial production.

Manufacturers also turned their attention to tree decorations in the latter half of the 19th century. Many exquisite glass and fabric ornaments were imported from Germany – notably baubles, bells, beaded balls, gold and silver stars and tiny stuffed toys and Santas.

Right: We decorated the blue spruce Christmas tree in The Red Sitting Room at Sissinghurst with a red star (spray-painted), tartan bows, green and red fleur-de-lys, polystyrene rings wrapped with red and gold brocade ribbons, lavender-filled tartan boots, wooden beads, a Santa Claus and a selection of hand-painted plastic balls and hearts. (For suppliers of traditional tree decorations, see The Directory, pages 157–158.)

However, many people continued to make their own ornaments. The practical household guides of the time gave instructions for making paper boxes, cones and drums to hold sugar plums, along with ideas for hand-made baubles and lanterns. In this chapter we have included illustrations and instructions showing you how to make two traditional Victorian tree decorations – a lantern and an orb (*see* pages 68–69). However, there is also a wide range of commercially available tree decorations, both traditional and modern, natural and man-made (for suppliers, *see* The Directory, pages 157–158), which should provide plenty of inspiration.

Whether we are spending Christmas in London or Kent, we invariably have two trees in the house. At Sissinghurst, our country home, we decorate the tree in the inglenook with garlands of seashells, pine cones, cinnamon sticks tied with wheat-ears or raffia, and candles – natural decorations in keeping with the house, while the tree in The Red Sitting Room there always has a tartan theme – something I insist on, being a Scot. At Eldon Lodge, our Victorian house in town, we often copy a decorative scheme from a Victorian Christmas card when dressing the main tree – gold ribbons, Victorian cut-outs, painted and gilt glass balls and the like predominating, although some years we simply take a festive colour theme, such as red, green or gold, as our starting point. The children also have their own small tree – edible decorations such as cookies, strings of popcorn and tissue-wrapped sweets being their favourites.

Finally, nowadays there is quite a broad selection of trees to choose from – many importers and retailers having become more adventurous as far as different species are concerned. We have included advice on choosing a tree for Christmas on page 61.

Right: *We dressed the "The Gold Tree" at Eldon Lodge with chains, glass balls, comedy-tragedy masks, wooden stars, miniature musical instruments and icicles – all painted gold – and gold bows made up from some 100 metres (330ft) of gold metallic ribbon. We also added a small selection of reproduction Victorian cut-outs depicting children and animals.*

CHOOSING A TREE

Nowadays, garden centres and greengrocers stock a wide variety of species of Christmas tree. Each has its own characteristics with regard to shape, longevity and even smell. Among the most popular are: the Douglas Fir, which is symmetrically shaped and has long-lasting, short green needles; the Balsam Fir, which has unevenly spaced branches, long-lasting, shiny dark green needles and a pleasant fragrance; the symmetrically shaped Blue Spruce, with its short, sharp, dense bluish needles, which drop quite quickly; the bushy Norway Spruce, which has short dark green needles that also drop quickly; the long-lasting, thin-needled, bushy Eastern White Pine; and the Scots Pine, which has slender, dark blue-green needles that rarely drop.

Whichever species you opt for, the most important thing is to make sure it is fresh. A tired tree will drop its needles as soon as you bring it into a centrally heated environment. So, choose one with flexible branches, sturdy needles (which won't be dislodged by a good tug), and a trunk that is still sticky with sap.

As soon as you get your tree home, remove any protective covering and store it outside until you are ready to bring it indoors. After you have set it up – in a tub packed with bricks and damp earth, or a tree-stand that holds water – spray the needles with water every day to maintain its condition. (Do not do this if you have hung electric lights from the branches!) Ideally, the tree should be kept in a cool room, but if your family objects to a Christmas spent in thermal layers you could turn the heating off only overnight. (A humidifier will also help.)

If you want to buy a rooted tree you can plant out and use again next year, look for a container-grown type. After Christmas, place it in a cool garage or basement for one week to condition it to lower temperatures. Then settle it into a pre-dug hole, loosening the compacted roots with a fork and packing the original earth, along with some compost, around the roots. Finally, stamp down the earth and water well.

Right: *"Happy Christmas" by Viggo Johansen (1851-1935), depicts a Victorian family holding hands around the Christmas tree. The tradition of lighting small wax tapers or candles on the tree on Christmas Eve, while all the family assembled, dates back to the middle of the 19th century. Because of the not inconsiderable risk of fire, the tapers or candles were only lit for a short while, and never left unattended.*

Left: *The large Christmas tree at Chilston was dressed with a selection of reproduction and antique Victorian tree decorations. Coloured glass baubles – single balls, bells, bunches of grapes and strands of beads – were combined with antique fabric slippers, cornets, lanterns and orbs. To complete the effect, mauve silk ribbons were trailed down the branches from elaborate bows at the top of the tree*

Right: *Antique glass baubles such as this one, hand-painted in a rich paisley design, are particularly appropriate for decorating a traditional Victorian-style Christmas tree; as are ropes of colourful glass beads.*

Don't despair if you are unable to track down original antique examples. A very similar effect can be created by using glossy-painted, papier mâché balls. These are imported from India, are widely available and relatively inexpensive.

Below: *These miniature tartan bootees – a traditional novelty shape dating back to the 19th century – are filled with lavender and designed to scent the Christmas tree. As an alternative to lavender, you could fill them with pot-pourri (for recipes see page 87).*

Above: *Tiny pale mauve and silver baubles, bunched to imitate grapes.* Below: *Thumb-nail-size comedy and tragedy masks provide a touch of theatre.*

Above: *Reproductions of Victorian decorations: a scrap-style motif made from laminated card (top) and a doll-sized slipper made from antique fabric and braid (bottom).*

Left: *The glass bauble was first mass-produced during the 19th century in jewel-bright colours. The more costly versions were made in novelty shapes, such as bells, and were hand-painted. Similar baubles are still made in the same way today, and some suppliers stock antique examples.*

Right: *Decorations created from antique fabrics like this braided Victorian-style orb (for instructions* see *pages 68–69) are easy to make at home.*

Right: *Original hand-painted Victorian and Edwardian glass bells are still available, at a price, from a few specialist suppliers. High-quality reproductions are easier to obtain.*

Right: *Fleurs-de-lis and cherubs are classic motifs widely used to embellish traditional Christmas decorations.*

Below:*A generous number of bows, made from the same richly coloured or metallic wired ribbon, are a simple and relatively inexpensive way to create a special scheme for a tree. Wind fine-gauge florist's wire around the middle of each bow, twisting the ends together at the back and then using them to attach the bows securely to the branches.*

Since the 19th century, tartan fabrics, like the bow above, and Santas, like the figure below, have played an important role in the imagery of Christmas.

Right: *Victorians made fabric-wrapped card cornets like this home-made version, covered with antique fabric, to fill with sugar-plums and hang from the tree.*

CHRISTMAS COOKIES

Each year we have a children's Christmas tea party. Cara and Kirsty help in the kitchen and decorate a small tree, hanging cookies, sweets and small presents from the branches – a custom that originated in Austria and Germany. If you have dogs in the house, make sure the tree is out of their reach. On more than one occasion Digby, a Spandoodle with no regard for party etiquette, has overturned the tree, savaged the presents and gorged himself on the cookies – much to the delight, it must be said, of the children.

85g/3oz butter, softened
125g/4oz caster sugar
1 small egg, plus 1 egg yolk
175g/6oz flour
glacé icing
sugar balls and jelly cake decorations
Makes about 20 cookies

1 Cream the butter and sugar until it is light and fluffy. Mix in the eggs and then gradually add the flour. Having brought the dough together with your hands, roll it out to a thickness of about ½cm/⅕in. Cut out the shapes either with cookie cut-

ters or the top of a glass jar. If you wish to hang them on the Christmas tree, make a small hole near one end with a skewer or knitting needle.

2 Transfer the cookies to a baking sheet and bake in a preheated oven at 180°C/350°F/Gas Mark 4, for 10-20 minutes, until they are golden brown. Remove from the oven, place on a wire rack and leave to cool. (*Note:* you may need to remake the holes at this point, before they have cooled.)

Decorate the cookies by first dipping them into glacé icing.

3 Next, stick the sugar balls and jelly decorations onto the icing arranging them either at random or in patterns as you wish.

4 Provided the dog hasn't beaten you to it, hang the cookies on the tree (as *opposite*) by simply threading lengths of red ribbon through the holes, tying them with simple bows and looping over the branches.

Instead of hanging tinsel or ribbon around the tree in the inglenook at Sissinghurst, we wound delicate garlands of seashells culled from the beach in the summer, and the tree was subtly lit by a collection of small beeswax candles clipped to the branches with small brass candle-holders. Cinnamon sticks from the kitchen jar were bundled together with wheat-ears and secured to the branches with a twist of raffia topped by mini pine cones *(top left). The orange slices (top right) were bought from a specialist supplier but you can make them yourself by baking in an oven until hard. We raided the store cupboard to make the delicate bunches of saucer-shaped dried mushrooms (bottom right). The fabric robins perched on the boughs (bottom left) were also bought from a specialist supplier.*

1

2

VICTORIAN ORB

I made this delightful Victorian tree decoration, together with the lantern below, for next to nothing, using mostly bits and pieces from my workbox.

MATERIALS

Paper; scissors; tape measure; glue; polystyrene ball; fabric scraps; silver braid; gold rick-rack braid; pins; silver and gold sequins; rocaille beads; medium-gauge florist's wire; assorted beads; narrow ribbon.

1 The ball is covered by four oval scraps of fabric. To size a paper template, measure the circumference of the ball and divide in half for the length and by four for the width. Using the template, cut two ovals from one fabric and two ovals from

VICTORIAN LANTERN

MATERIALS

Scissors; needle; thimble; iron; tape measure; pen; thick card; button thread; iron-on interfacing; plain and patterned fabrics; glue; narrow

gold braid; pins; rocaille and faceted coloured glass beads.

1 Cut four equal-sized isosceles triangles from thick card. Cut four equal-sized equilateral triangles, the sides of which

must be the same length as the bases of the isosceles triangles. Iron interfacing onto the wrong sides of both fabrics. Place two isosceles and two equilateral triangles on the wrong side of the plain fabric, and the remaining four on the patterned

1

2

another, and glue alternately to the ball.

2 Cut two lengths of silver metallic braid just longer than the circumference. Wrap tightly around the ball, covering joins between fabrics and fixing with a pin just off-centre at the top. Repeat with gold

rick-rack, dividing each quarter into half.

3 Make a small loop at one end of a length of florist's wire. Thread on a large glass bead and sequin. Push the wire through the ball and thread on more beads. Trim the wire, leaving enough to make a loop.

4 Take 16 pins, thread a rocaille bead and a small sequin on to each one and push them through the silver braid, centring on the sides of the ball in groups of four. Finally, tie narrow ribbon through the top loop of the wire, and hang from a tree.

---

fabric. Mark around each triangle with a pen. Allowing a ½cm/¼in turn-in, cut out the eight fabric triangles, glue the card templates within the penmarks, fold back the turn-ins and glue.

2 Using overcast stitch and alternating

fabrics, sew the sides of the isosceles triangles together, then those of the equilaterals, to form two pyramids. Next sew the bases of the pyramids together.

3 Position gold braid along the edges of the lantern – verticals first, horizontals

second – and pin at the corners.

4 Thread a number of pins with a rocaille bead and insert at intervals along the gold braid. Stitch loops of rocaille and faceted beads to the top and bottom corners, and tassels of the same to the others.

PRESENTS

The tradition of giving gifts on Christmas Eve or Christmas Day really began in Victorian times. Before that, presents were exchanged at New Year or on Saint Nicolas's Day (December 6th). Presents were often of clothing. For example, in 1579 Queen Elizabeth I received a satin nightgown and a sea-water green satin petticoat from Sir Francis Walsingham. She also was given "aids to toilet", such as tooth picks and ear picks made from precious metals and encrusted with jewels. Elizabethan gifts among families and friends often included a hogshead of claret, a basket of apples, oysters and puddings – such collections being the forerunners of the present-day Christmas hamper.

While the early Victorians didn't receive many presents, by the end of the 19th century Christmas had become almost as commercial as it is today. From the beginning of November onwards, many shops were full of Christmas wares and the streets were crowded with shoppers, while catalogues and advertisements in magazines offered merchandise by post to those who couldn't make the journey into town. The range of goods available was impressive – in 1887 one trader alone was offering 100,000 gift ideas to potential customers. Presents for adults ranged from silver candlesticks to ribbon bookmarks. Personal accessories were common – silver-backed hairbrushes, chatelaine bags, dressing cases, scent bottles, workboxes and fans for ladies, cigarette cases, fob watches and shaving implements for men.

The Victorians were not averse to gimmicky novelties. Small gifts such as pincushions, for example, were sold in a myriad of shapes and materials – from silver shoes with cushion tops to velvet stars or ribbonwork rosettes studded with pins. Other items included match stands in the shape of solid silver boots and cigar lighters manufactured to look like table lamps. And jewellery was manufactured in novelty shapes, such as brooches in the form of cats, dogs, and seasonal sprig of mistletoe.

Like today, gifts for children were a major part of the festival. Museums full of Victorian toys attest to the large-scale production that took place to meet the demand. Rare and highly collectable, when toys such as Stieff teddy-bears and Britains' hand-painted lead soldiers appear at auction nowadays they command prices well beyond the pocket of any child and most parents too.

Many inventive and mechanically sophisticated toys were sold, most of the best examples coming from manufacturers in Germany such as Lehmann or Bing. Presents for both boys and girls included mechanical trains and boats, automata such as animals dancing or playing musical instruments and singing birds in cages. Also a wide range of board games, such as "snakes and ladders" and "tiddlywinks", were bought as Christmas presents.

Right: Victorian-style "keepsake" boxes and presents, wrapped in traditional plain and patterned papers and embellished with decorative ribbons, braids, rosettes and bows, under the tree at Chilston.

Above: "Christmas Eve" by Walter Anderson (1856-86).

Victorian boys of well-to-do parents built up collections of the ubiquitous toy soldiers, while girls could acquire a wonderful selection of wax and china dolls, complete with wardrobes of clothes. One doll advertised at Christmas was "Miss Dollie Dimple", who was sold complete with a travelling trunk full of clothes for only one shilling. Many of these dolls came from factories in France and Germany, notably Jumeau, Bru and Kammer.

The Victorians also excelled at making doll's houses, which were often architecturally perfect copies of actual dwellings, both grand and humble. Miniature shops, theatres, zoos, farms and forts were also made. These came with all the accoutrements needed to play at shopkeeper, producer, zookeeper, farmer or General.

Not all gifts were bought, however. Just as today, the Victorians enjoyed giving and receiving home-made presents. Many magazines and household guides gave instructions on how to make chocolates, samplers, needlework items, pressed flower pictures or hair "paintings". Children's sweets or toys were often hand-made by mother or sister; craft skills such as embroidery, découpage (*see* pages 96–97) and crochetwork, so valued in the young women of the day, being pressed into use.

Our own children enjoy making presents – as I do – and the recipients always seem to appreciate the thought and care that goes into them far more than they would any hastily bought trinket. In this chapter we show and explain how to make a variety of gifts, including edible presents such as chocolate truffles (*see* pages 80–81), preserved and caramelized fruits, herb oils and vinegars and Christmas cookies (*see* pages 82–83). We have also included a number of recipes for making your own festive potpourris (*see* pages 86–87), which can be used around the house as well as given as presents. In the case of the latter, I always try to make sachets and bags for the potpourris (or lavender) from scraps of antique lace or embroidery, which can be picked up quite cheaply in boxes of "odds" at auction and lend gifts a traditional air rarely matched by modern fabrics.

Below: "Presents for the children from the tree" (1852) by H.J. Schneider.

If you don't have time to exercise your artistic talents, theme presents are another way of introducing a personal touch. For example, for a keen gardener you could fill a wooden trug with packets of unusual seeds, reels of twine and old-fashioned terracotta flower pots. For a cook buy a traditional mixing bowl and pile in twists of spices, cinnamon sticks, whole grain mustard, comb honey, crystallized fruit and the finest balsamic vinegar.

"Children with their presents" by Ida Waugh (c.1890)

For traditionalists of all ages, fill baskets or pretty boxes with timeless presents, such as glass beads, lace hankies and diamanté hairclips for women, and wooden soldiers, classic storybooks and a sturdy sailboat for boys.

Giving presents is, in many respects, rather like offering someone a meal: the art lies as much in the presentation as the content. A wonderful selection of fancy wrapping papers, ribbons, paper cut-outs and traditional Christmas stockings are available from department stores and specialist suppliers (*see* The Directory, pages 157–158). They can be used in a variety of ways to embellish all manner of gifts. Numerous examples can be seen throughout the chapter, which you can either copy or draw on for inspiration. Alternatively, you might prefer to design your own wrapping paper (*see* pages 92–93).

Finally, being so closely associated with the world of collecting, Martin and I naturally like to give antiques as Christmas presents. Many people are intimidated by the thought of buying antiques for themselves, let alone other people, particularly in relation to the cost. However, virtually all of the presents we give at Christmas were purchased at bargain prices at auctions either some time ago or during the previous year. On pages 76–79 we have included a small selection of antique presents and described where and when we bought them and how much they cost us. We hope this will inspire you with new ideas for Christmas presents and, if you have not already done so, venture into the exciting world of antiques and collectables.

Below: *"Fruit from the Christmas tree" – a sketch at the foundling hospital, Guildford street – from a picture by Arthur Hopkins (1881).*

ANTIQUE PRESENTS

Martin and I often give antiques and collectables as Christmas presents. Although largely confined to adult friends and relatives, we also give them to children. For example, a few years ago I introduced two of my godchildren to the joys of collecting antiques by giving one a 19th-century Staffordshire pastille burner and the other a handful of post-First World War military postcards, and have added to them subsequently.

Although we buy most of these gifts at auctions, a fair number are picked up at boot fairs, jumble sales and antique and charity shops, almost always at bargain prices. Perhaps the best piece of advice we could give to anyone contemplating buying at auction is to check out the piece in question very carefully before bidding, set yourself a sensible price limit and don't go beyond it, even if sorely tempted in the excitement of the moment. (*Miller's Antiques Price Guides, Collectables Price Guides* and *Checklists* will be of great assistance to you, as they contain a wealth of information on antiques and their value.) We hope the eclectic selection of antiques compiled by Martin and myself – shown on the previous pages and described here – provides you with ideas for presents for your own family and friends.

1 Leather-bound books always make a good present, especially if you can find an author or a subject of particular interest to the recipient. Antiquarian book shops are the prime source for first editions in pristine condition, although these can prove to be a very expensive present nowadays. Nevertheless, it is possible to pick up less-than-perfect copies for £15–£30, or even less if you come across them at boot fairs, jumble sales or charity shops.

2 The price of late 19th-/early 20th-century Chinese blue and white joss stick holders is always dependent on the quality of the painting. Well-painted figures and animals are particularly desirable and can fetch £100–£150 at auction. However, the examples here were bought in a lot of ten for £60. Given that few people actually know what they are, they often turn up in junk shops for a few pounds.

3 We bought this late 19th-century pewter tankard for £18. Undistinguished pewter is often sold in mixed lots at auction and frequently sells very cheaply.

4 A late 19th-century Staffordshire teacup and saucer, bought in a job-lot at auction. Prices vary considerably, depending on the factory, condition and decoration, but you can expect to pay £10–£20 for a simply decorated pair.

5 We bought this set of late 19th-century porcelain coffee cups and saucers, with good quality blue decoration and gilding, at a house sale for approximately £20.

6 A late 19th-century Wedgwood agate ware tankard with silver-plated mounts would fetch over £200 at auction if perfect. However, this example had a crack running from top to bottom and cost £40.

7 Late 19th-century polychrome Chinese tiles were mass-produced for the European market, so there are a lot about. They are usually sold in lots at auction, and we paid £100 for 20, one example of which is shown here. Tiles make a particularly nice present when framed (see the four above the painting in the background), as do prints, which can often be bought quite cheaply in portfolios at auction. For example, I bought some lovely 19th-century Japanese prints for only £8 in this way – although it cost a further £8 to have each one framed.

8 This early 20th-century silver-plated powder flask cost £10–£12 and is an ideal present for a gun enthusiast.

9 Although a late 19th-century treen glove powderer, such as the one here, could fetch £40–£60 at auction, treen items often turn up unrecognized at jumble sales and can be bought for a few pounds.

10 Although pieces of treenware are now highly collectable, Martin picked up this 19th-century coquilla nut nutmeg grater in a job-lot of "wooden bits" in a London antiques market for £20. Its actual value now is £80–£100.

11 This modern copy of an 18th-century turned wooden (red walnut) bobbin stand was made by a friend in Rye, and cost £30.

12 A 1st-century AD Roman glass flask, probably from a burial site. Unless in particularly fine condition, such antiquities are not that sought after and can be picked up for £30–£40.

13 The price of Victorian pictures created from plaited human hair cuttings, is very much dependent on condition and how pleasing the design is. This example would fetch £200–£400.

14 The cracked handle and slightly chipped spout enabled us to buy this late 19th-century silver lustre jug for £25. If perfect it would have gone for far more.

15 Late 19th-century magnifying glasses with mahogany handles, such as the one here, can be found at £10–£15. However, you should beware of similar glasses made from old knife handles.

16 This 19th-century French mahogany mantel clock is worth as much as £300–£400. Mantel clocks vary enormously in value, depending on condition, movement (whether it is in working order and who the maker was) and style. The popularity of Gothic style, especially when the details are finely executed as in this example, explains the high price.

17 Antique corkscrews make excellent presents, and late 19th-century and early 20th-century examples actually work better than their modern counterparts. Very unusual designs and ingenious shapes fetch several hundred pounds, but simple screws can be bought for anything between £10–£40.

18 This late 19th-century brass inkwell is worth £25–£30 but, like many brass items, could be picked up for far less outside the antique trade – at a boot fair or jumble sale, for example.

19 & 20 These two modern copies of Chinese blue and white ceramics cost approximately £20–£30 each.

21 Buying part Victorian dinner services at auction can prove a cost-effective way of buying presents in bulk. I picked up a quite impressive Imari pattern, 20-piece set for £200.

22 Although actually worth £20–£25, I've seen these late 19th-century Staffordshire spongeware jugs turn up for a few pounds in junk shops. This is partly due to the fact that unless you know what they are they look quite modern.

23 Export ware blue and white Chinese porcelain, such as this bowl and cover, has been imported into Europe in vast quantities, particularly during the late 19th and early 20th centuries. Such pieces can still be bought for £5–£10, depending on condition and the quality of the design and painting.

24 A late 19th-century Chinese *famille verte* baluster vase such as this would fetch £400–£600 if perfect, but half that if imperfect.

25 We picked up this 19th-century maple-framed engraving for £30. However, as an alternative you can buy modern books of prints and artificially age them with tea (without the milk) before having them framed. The cost of a modern print works out at 50p–£1, and an antique frame anything from £1 upwards.

26 Worth £20–£30, this Edwardian brass tobacco box is engraved: "A still tongue makes a wise head".

27 A modern reproduction, wooden decoy duck, worth £20–£25.

28 You can pick up Goss and crested ware gifts, such as this dog and kennel, for as little as £3–£6.

1

2

3

CHOCOLATE TRUFFLES

As an alternative to buying chocolates at Christmas, the children and I often prepare them ourselves. You can serve these delicious chocolate truffles on a decorative plate at tea or after dinner. When presented in a simple box lined with gold tissue paper, trimmed with ruched ribbon and braid and sealed with wax, they also make a luxury gift, especially when laced with whisky or cognac.

4

5 tablespoons double cream
600g/1¼lb plain chocolate, broken into
  small pieces
1–2 tablespoons whisky or cognac (optional)
4 tablespoons cocoa powder (for dusting)
Makes 350g/12oz – approx 16 chocolates

1 Pour the cream into a small saucepan and heat gently until it is tepid. Put 250g/8oz of the chocolate pieces into a small basin and melt gently over hot, but not boiling water, stirring occasionally. Do not let the bottom of the basin sit in the hot water as it is essential that the chocolate does not overheat.

2 When the chocolate has melted, remove the bowl from the heat and slowly pour in the cream in a gentle trickle, stirring thoroughly to mix.

3 Let the mixture cool a little and add whisky or cognac if you wish. Whisk with a balloon or electric whisk until the mixture becomes lighter in colour and stands in peaks. (This may take 3 or 4 minutes.) Then place in the refrigerator for about 20 minutes, until stiff.

4 Sieve the cocoa powder onto a tray or board. Remove spoonfuls of the chocolate paste and roll into balls about 2½cm/1in in diameter. Drop each ball into the cocoa powder and roll to cover. Then leave the balls in a cool place until firm.

5 To cover the truffle balls in chocolate, melt the remaining 350g/12oz of plain chocolate over hot water. Spear each truffle on a skewer, dip them one by one into the melted chocolate and place them on a marble slab or tin foil to set.

5

EDIBLE PRESENTS

When Christmas closes in, I often find that I still have some gifts to buy for relatives and friends but am running out of time and inspiration. In this situation, delicious edible presents are the perfect solution, and being simple to make, preparing them is much more fun than struggling around overcrowded department stores at the last moment. What's more, jars of fruits in alcohol, flavoured oils, special preserves, chocolate truffles, fruits dipped in chocolate and cookies convey the personal touch if they have been made by hand and packed into an unusual pot or dish discovered on one of our antique-hunting forays.

HERB OILS

Almost any herbs can be macerated in olive or sunflower oils to make an aromatic oil. Basil, thyme and rosemary are particularly suitable.

Rinse the herbs gently under running water. Shake them dry and put them into clean jars or bottles. Pour over olive or sunflower oil to the top and seal thoroughly. Leave for two weeks before using.

HERB AND FLOWER VINEGARS

Any white or red wine vinegar can be flavoured with herbs or flowers. Try adding rosemary sprigs or lavender flowers to bottles of white wine vinegar. Leave them in a sunny place until the herbs have scented the oil.

Rose petals can be used to great effect to make a refreshing flower vinegar. Add highly scented rose petals (shop-bought ones may still be covered with insecticides) to wine vinegar. Leave in a sunny place until they have coloured the vinegar. Use on leafy salads.

PRESERVED FRUITS

Fruits preserved in brandy or eau-de-vie can be served as a dessert, with or without cream. Spoon plenty of the bottling liquid, which will have taken up some of the fruit flavour, over the fruit as you serve. Keep the fruits covered with liquor at all times. Red or golden fruits make particularly beautiful gifts.

2kg/4lb fresh fruits, cherries, raspberries,
*   peaches*
2 litres/3¹/₂ pints eau-de-vie or brandy
cinnamon sticks
cloves
500g/1lb sugar

Pack the fruit with the spices into spotlessly clean kilner jars. Melt the sugar over a low heat with just enough water to cover. Add the alcohol to the syrup and pour over the fruits. Seal the jars and store for a week or so before eating.

FRUITS DIPPED IN CHOCOLATE

500g/1lb large strawberries
350g/12oz cherries
500g/1lb kumquats
500g/1lb plain chocolate, chopped
1 teaspoon sunflower oil

Melt the chocolate in a basin over hot water, making sure that it does not get too hot. Stir in the sunflower oil.

Dip the fruits into the melted chocolate and place on greaseproof paper to set. Carefully peel the fruits off the paper and place into paper cases.

CHRISTMAS COOKIES

For recipe, *see* page 65.

GILDED GINGERBREAD

Since medieval times gilded gingerbread has been a popular gift. Traditionally, the dark ground of the bread was studded with gilded fleurs-de-lis made from box leaves, through which cloves were pushed to resemble nails. Over the years the basic ingredients have varied. For example, lighter versions of the traditional recipe given here included eggs and cream or milk, and white icing has provided an alternative means of decoration since the early 19th century.

1.4kg/3¹/₂lb plain flour
¹/₂kg/1¹/₂lb honey
200g/7oz butter
¹/₂ whole nutmeg, grated
1 tablespoon ground ginger
1 teaspoon baking powder
1 egg, separated
1–2 sheets gold leaf

Melt the honey and butter in a little hot water. Mix in the dry ingredients. Knead and roll out the dough on a baking sheet. Bake for about 20 minutes in a cool oven set at 180°C/350°F/Gas Mark 4. Decorate immediately, pressing on the gold leaf while the cake is still hot (for method, *see* page 134). You may need to use the white of the egg to help the gold leaf adhere.

Lavender or pot-pourri-filled sachets are inexpensive gifts that the children find easy to make. They use antique lace cloths or mats picked up at charity shops or flea markets. Well-laundered, these are then simply seamed on three sides to make a bag, filled and tied at the neck with ribbon or lace.

As part of the house decorations for Christmas I fill antique bowls, such as the ones overleaf. Open bowls have been used to display pot-pourri since the 19th century; before then ceramic jars were used. These had an openwork lid which was covered during the day by a solid top lid. Once evening fell, the jar was placed on the hearth and turned until warm. The lid was then removed, releasing the perfume. This system kept the fragrance remarkably well, the jar being refilled only once a year, about a month before Christmas.

POT-POURRI

We fill bowls of all kinds, large and small, old and new, with pot-pourri to scent the house for Christmas. I find making up these traditional recipes infinitely preferable and more satisfying to buying many of the commercially available varieties.

ENGLISH ROSE POT-POURRI
3 large cups dried rose petals
2 large cups lavender flowers
1 large cup scented leaves (try bay, sweet myrtle and scented geranium)
1 tablespoon powdered allspice
1 tablespoon coarse-ground or finely broken cinnamon
¹/₂ tablespoon powdered cloves
14g/¹/₂oz powdered orris root
7g/¹/₄oz powdered gum benzoin
7ml/¹/₄floz good rose pot-pourri essence

CHRISTMAS POT-POURRI
1 tablespoon grated orange peel
1 large cup dried pine needles or dried herbs
6 cups assorted small pine cones, barks, dry leaves and seedheads
1 cup dried rose petals (preferably red)
2 tablespoons crushed cinnamon
2 tablespoons whole allspice
2 tablespoons ground nutmeg
¹/₂ tablespoon whole cloves (more if required)
2 tablespoons ground orris root
1 tablespoon powdered gum benzoin
20 drops orange oil
20 drops rose oil
20 drops cinnamon oil
10 drops bergamot oil
10 drops myrrh (optional)

WOODLAND POT-POURRI
2 cups fir cones
¹/₂ cup beech mast
Sprigs of blue and green fir
1 cup dried or glycerined leaves
1 cup bark or lichen seedheads
1 cup seasonal dried flowers
Dried peel from 4 or 5 large oranges
56g/2oz star anise
28g/1oz allspice berries
14g/¹/₂oz cloves
6 cinnamon sticks
1 tablespoon orris powder
1 tablespoon ground nutmeg
1 tablespoon ground cinnamon
1 tablespoon ground cloves
14g/¹/₂oz powdered gum benzoin
20 drops cedarwood oil
15 drops cinnamon oil
10 drops oil of cloves
25 drops orange oil
10 drops frankincense (optional)

To mix the pot-pourris, gently combine all the dried plant material in a very large bowl, then mix in the spices, orris powder and gum benzoin and finally the fragrant oil, a drop at a time. Stir the whole together.

Seal the pot-pourri in a glazed earthenware crock or a stoppered glass jar. If you don't have either of these you can use a turkey roasting bag as an alternative. However, you should avoid metal or plastic containers as they can "leach" the perfume.

Cure for up to six weeks (you must allow a minimum of at least two weeks) in a warm and dry, dark place. Shake gently from time to time to blend.

LADY BETTY GERMAIN'S POT-POURRI
This recipe, revived by Gertrude Jekyll in *Home and Garden* (1900), dates from *c.* 1750. Exact quantities for flowers and herbs were never given as amounts depended on what you had in your garden.

Double violets
Rose leaves
Lavender
Myrtle flowers
Verbena
Bay leaves
Rosemary
Balm
Geranium
Cinnamon
Mace
Nutmeg
Pepper
Bay salt
Pounded lemon peel
200g/¹/₂lb orris root
28g/1oz storax
28g/1oz gum Benjamin
56g/2oz Calamino aromatico
2g/0.07oz musk
a few drops of oil of Rhodium

Gather the herbs and flowers when dry, picking them from the stalks and drying them on paper in the sun for a day or two before putting them into a covered jar and layering with bay salt. Cut a piece of card to the exact size of the jar and keep this pressed down on the flowers. Add the spices and gums, mix all well together with a new wooden spoon, press down well and spread bay salt on top. Store in a cool, dry place for several months.

PRESENTING CANDLES

Candles have always been an essential part of a traditional Christmas celebration. The rich warm glow of candlelight just cannot be matched by electric lighting, however sophisticated. Moreover, the subtle honeyed scent given off by candles with a high beeswax content adds to the festive atmosphere. (You should avoid candles with a high percentage of paraffin wax as they emit a rather unpleasant smell when burning.) Consequently, Martin and I use candles for both illumination and decoration throughout the house over Christmas, although for safety's sake we always make a point of never leaving them alight and unattended.

Of course, candles also make wonderful presents, and even the largest ones won't make too great a dent in your purse. They are most effective as gifts if you put a little time and effort into their presentation, rather than simply bundling them into plain wrapping paper.

Whichever way you decide to wrap them, you must ensure that they are securely held in position; left loose they may rattle against each other and become damaged. For example, the beeswax candles shown *left* were bound together with a handsome tie made from purple, ruched satin ribbon and gold furnishing braid.

The selection of ribbed and red and gold and green and gold Gothic candles *above left* were cushioned on a bed of green velvet used to line a gold card box. A frill of green, ruched satin ribbon, secured with gold furnishing braid, and a gold wire-edged Paisley bow add the finishing touch to this glamorous present.

The small candle display *above right* was created by securing the bases of the tapered candles to an oval block of florist's dry foam (for technique, *see* page 114). Tissue paper was fixed around the block with dried flower heads wired to the foam, and decorative folds of tissue and scrolls of reproduction Victorian music were pressed in around the bases of the candles.

Dear Father
CHristmas.

plis may I have
A doLL with
Long hair
A musical box

The custom of hanging stockings over the mantel, near the chimney or at the foot of the bed to fill with small presents for the children of the house is thought to have its origins in the tale of St Nicolas, who was the Bishop of Myra in Asia Minor in the 4th century. According to the legend, this wealthy prelate threw three bags of gold through the window of an impoverished family in order to provide dowries for their daughters. The bags are said to have fallen into the girl's stockings, which were hung up by the fire to dry. The custom of hanging up a Christmas stocking, and the identity of one of its traditional ingredients, chocolate coins, commemorates this legend. Because the stockings were hanging by the fire, the belief grew up that Santa's secret route into the house was via the chimney.

In the 19th century, Christmas stockings were often made from everyday pairs, outgrown by the youngest of the children in the family. They were embellished with embroidered designs and fancy trimmings and filled with penny toys and sweets. Later in the century, mothers made stockings in Berlin woolwork or needlepoint, decorated with Santas and mottoes. If you want to follow suit, patterns based on the original Victorian designs are available from specialist outlets today.

Our children's country Christmas stockings are made from homespun cotton in Shaker style; in London they have Victorian needlepoint versions. On Christmas Eve, before the children go to bed, they hang up their stockings by the fireside. Anticipating Santa's visit, they leave a note listing their Christmas requests and a glass of refreshment on the mantel covered with a lace doily. (Sherry and a mince pie are traditional, but Sissinghurst's Santa prefers whisky.)

When the children come down early on Christmas morning they find that the stockings have been filled with a selection of traditional goodies (*see* right) and the whisky has disappeared. The small gifts in the stockings keep the children occupied and (reasonably) happy until it is time to open one or two of their larger presents after breakfast.

TRADITIONAL STOCKING FILLERS

When we assemble traditional stockings for our children, we start by filling the toe with an apple, which is supposed to symbolize good health, and then drop an orange and a nut into the heel (in earlier times, these were rare and costly treats).

Next, we add some timeless toys – for example, wooden whistles or tops, or tiny cloth dolls – and one or two handfuls of home-made sweets, such as toffee or peppermint drops, wrapped in cellophane and tied with ribbon.

As well as some chocolate money, we also include a real coin fresh from the mint as tradition has it that this is a symbol of future wealth. We then pack in a few more nuts and oranges, then finally we add a twist of salt for good luck.

However, there is one traditional ingredient we leave out because we don't think our children appreciate finding it in their stockings on Christmas morning – it's a lump of coal, which is said to guarantee warmth for years to come.

HOME-MADE WRAPPING PAPER

Rather than buy wrapping paper and gift tags, Cara designed her own using a wood block stamp and gold powder, both of which are available from craft shops.

MATERIALS

Brown wrapping paper; plain square box; angel stamp and ink pad; sheet of coloured cartridge paper; candle (or table lamp); gold or bronze metallic powder; small bowl or saucer; shot silk or cotton ribbon; scissors; clear Sellotape.

1 Cut the wrapping paper to size. Then lay it flat on the table and stamp the angel print either at regular intervals or at random over the surface.

2 Wrap the paper round the box, securing in position with clear Sellotape.

KEEPSAKE BOX

Using gold spray paint and ribbon and braid, a plain oval box can be easily transformed into an elegant gift wrapping that's a keepsake in its own right.

MATERIALS

Oval cardboard or wooden box; gold spray paint; 7½cm/3in wide stiff polyester moiré ribbon; 6¼cm/2½ in gold-edged black gauze ribbon; decorative gold braid; double-sided adhesive tape; PVA adhesive; scissors.

1 Pressing the adhesive tape against the back of the moiré ribbon, make a series of pleats two fingers deep until the ribbon is 1¼cm/½in longer than the box rim.

2 Stick adhesive tape on top of the ribbon and remove the backing. Centre the gold-

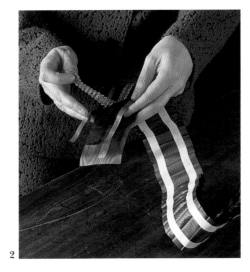

3 Cut a simple greeting tag from the cartridge paper and stamp an angel print on one side of it. Then, while the ink is still wet, sprinkle gold powder over it and shake the excess off into a bowl. Repeat until the print is completely covered.

4 To burnish the gold powder, hold the tag for roughly 30 seconds some 10cm/4in over a candle flame. Make sure you don't set the tag alight! (You can burnish the powder over a light bulb, but it takes up to 5 minutes to do it this way.)

5 Wrap the ribbon lengthways round the present. Then make a slit in the end of the tag and thread the ribbon through it so the tag is centred over the top of the box.
6 Twist the ribbon round the sides of the present and tie with a simple bow on top.

---

edged gauze over the tape and press into place. Repeat with the gold braid.
3 Remove the backing from the adhesive tape applied in step 1. Centre and secure the ribbon around the sprayed gold box, glueing the overlap at one end.

4 Make two loops of moiré ribbon; one half the length of the box, the other just over half the length of the box. Cut the shorter loop into two, then glue both halves inside the longer loop with roughly half their widths showing on either side.

Then repeat for the other side of the box.
5 Make a centre for the bow using the method described in steps 1-2, but this time reducing the size of the pleats.
6 Finally, fold the edges of the pleated ribbon under and glue into position.

Left: *The square box was wrapped in plum-coloured paper and trimmed with a silk bow, bunches of glass grapes and an ostrich feather, giving it a fin-de-siècle look, while the oval painted wooden box was embellished with ribbon, silk taffeta roses and gold paper leaves.*

Top: *Antique and modern trims were combined to create two Victorian-looking presents. Two antique silk ribbons encircle a velvet-covered box topped with ruffled silk taffeta ribbon (right), while an antique trim is paired with taffeta ribbon and paisley paper (left).*

Bottom left: *Velvet ribbon sewn with jewelled lozenges was used to tie up an antique doily for a wrap that becomes part of the gift.*
Bottom right: *A home-made cracker (see pages 112–113) makes a festive wrap for a small gift, such as a locket.*

1

2

3

4

DECOUPAGE

Découpage, the art of cutting out scraps of colourful paper and arranging them into collages to decorate boxes, cards, furniture and other artefacts, has been a popular pastime since the 17th century. Simple and fun to do, découpage is a great way of decorating Christmas gift boxes, rather than simply wrapping them in paper. All the materials you need, including reproduction Victorian cut-outs, are available from craft shops and other suppliers (*see* The Directory).

MATERIALS

Cardboard box; matte black emulsion paint; matte red art paper; printed Victorian cut-outs; wallpaper paste (containing fungicide); scissors; fine- or medium-grade wire wool; water-based varnish white glue (PVA); glitter.

1 Paint the plain cardboard box with two coats of matte black emulsion paint and allow to dry. Then cut out strips of matte red art paper, cutting each strip into two triangular-shaped bands as shown.

2 Mix the wallpaper paste and soak the Victorian cut-outs and the triangular-shaped strips in it overnight. Stick the strips to the lid and base of the box as shown, and repeat with the cut-outs arranging according to taste. Allow to dry.

3 Mix the water-based (PVA) varnish and brush on the first coat in a series of single, slightly overlapping strokes. Allow to dry and then rub down with wire wool before applying a second coat. Repeat up to four or five times – the more coats you apply, the more lustrous the finish.

4 To give the découpage a more festive appearance, as I've done here, add a little glitter to the varnish before you apply it.

For young children, one of the most magical moments of Christmas is receiving and opening their presents from under the tree. Traditionally we hand most of them out after breakfast and in all the excitement make a point of writing down who received what and from whom. In the past, forgetting to do this has caused more than a few difficulties when it comes to writing thankyou letters later on.

TABLE DECORATIONS

Abundant arrangements of flowers, fruits, antiques and collectables always form the centrepiece of our Christmas tables. We try to make sure that the display looks good from all sides, not just one. And we set the table to include plenty of salt cellars, butter dishes and the like so that there is no need for family and guests to reach over the arrangement and risk knocking it over – this is particularly important as our settings invariably include candles.

China does not have to be from one service; we often use a mixture of pieces, picked up at auctions over the years in those lucky-dip boxes known as "odds", that look good together. This is an inexpensive and stylish way to cater for a large party without resorting to paper plates.

We try to tie china, cutlery, glasses, table linen and decorations to a single theme. We may use a collection of antique Coalport or Crown Derby china as a starting point for a Victorian table, or base our scheme around colours (claret-red and holly-green, burnished gold and snow white), using antiques from different periods. During the run-up to Christmas the children and I usually make crackers to match (*see* pages 112–113).

Crackers have formed part of a traditional Christmas since the 19th century, when they were first created by Tom Smith. On a visit to Paris in 1840 this London baker and confectioner was inspired by bonbon wrappings, adapting the idea to his own products on his return. At first he just included a love message, but later added an explosive snap and a paper hat.

No Christmas table is complete without a focal arrangement; we try a different style each year. It may be based around flowers, it could be a display of fruits, either on a cone (*see* pages 110–111) or heaped on to a glorious antique épergne, or it could be a topiary tree of the sort that the Victorians used to make. The choice partly depends on whether we are spending Christmas in our town house or in the country. Settings at Sissinghurst, in Kent, are fairly simple, but in the Gothic artist's studio of our London house Martin likes to create a grand theatrical arrangement. These elaborate confections of antiques, flowers and fruit may look dauntingly expensive, but they depend far more on quantity than perfection for their effect. Like Martin, you could use inexpensive reproduction or slightly damaged pieces picked up cheaply at auction to set the mood. To us, the value of this table decoration lies in the way that it captures the spirit of Christmas, rather than in its catalogue prices.

*Right: Table decorations and place settings for our annual Christmas
Eve supper – the centrepiece is a low, oval-shaped display of candles
and flowers, including Euphorbia Fulgens, Euphorbia Marginata,
Phalanopia orchids and "Nicole" roses, all secured in a block of
florist's dry foam (for technique, see pages 114–115).*

SETTING THE TABLE FOR CHRISTMAS LUNCH

For Christmas lunch Martin sets up a series of trestle tables (these can be bought or hired cheaply) and covers them with the largest textile he can find. Here he used an old rug, picked up at an auction for a few pounds. Provided it is reasonably clean, the condition of the rug doesn't matter as any holes can be covered by artfully placed decorative objects.

Martin then arranged a large display of Casablanca lilies at the heart of the table. He chose them because they are large enough not to get lost in the conglomeration of objects placed around them, but sufficiently "neutral" not to dominate. They are also associated with decadence – which is in keeping with this essentially Baroque-style table setting.

Next, Martin ranged a variety of 18th- and 19th-century wooden, painted and gilded candlestands around the flowers (supporting candles of various shapes and sizes, but all with a high beeswax content. Avoid a high paraffin content, as they smell unpleasant). Like the lilies, they were deliberately chosen for their height – the setting intentionally obscuring guests' views across the table. This is an ideal device for breaking up a large gathering into small groups and thereby creating an air of intimacy around the table.

With the flowers and candles in place, Martin set about adding small groups of artefacts, along with a generous scattering of various fruits, nuts and sweets. In much the same way as decorating the fireplace (*see* pages 50–51), the aim is to create a series of "still-lives" containing elements appropriate to the Christmas festival (or simply of interest in their own right). Above all, they are intended to provide something for guests to examine or discuss between courses or during lulls in the conversation.

Opposite top left: a 19th-century Gothic brass mantel clock and glass lustre candlestick; a blue and white Chinese bowl; 18th-century English drinking glasses; a 19th-century bronze of a reclining woman; and a 19th-century French ormolu candlestick. *Opposite top right*: 19th-century horn beakers; a reproduction 18th-century salt cellar; an 18th-century fruitwood goblet; a selection of 18th- and 19th-century leather-bound books; a Worcester bough pot (*c.*1850); and a Victorian wooden treasure chest.

Opposite bottom right: a late 19th-century carved Buddha (on an 18th-century servant's oak ale counter); a 19th-century silhouette of Napoleon; 19th-century legal documents; a Worcester chestnut basket (*c.*1770); a blue and white Chinese bowl (*c.*1680); and an 18th-century silver-rimmed coconut goblet. *Opposite bottom left*: a 19th-century French marble figure of a boy eating grapes, and a 19th-century blue and white Chinese dish.

While some of the antiques Martin used are quite valuable, many, such as the books and legal documents, can be picked up cheaply at auction. Also, good quality reproductions of many others, such as the candlesticks and ceramics, can be bought for a few pounds. In other words, it needn't cost a fortune to recreate such a dramatic display.

TABLE SETTINGS

Setting the table is a relatively new tradition, dating back only to the 18th century. Medieval tables, for example, were actually long, narrow boards set on movable trestles. The household supplied platters, which were made from bread – the original, ecologically sound, disposable party plate – in humbler abodes, from wood or pewter in more affluent homes and from gold or silver in the wealthiest castles and manor houses. Cutlery and drinking vessels were not, however, provided. Instead, each guest bought his or her own knife, spoon and drinking cup with them.

The first real dining table designed to a shape that was suitable for display as well as for the consumption of food, appeared in the 18th century. With the arrival of this new wide table, the concept of creating a decorative setting appeared. As a consequence, the burgeoning middle classes began to accumulate collections of silver, linen, glassware and china. And food began to be treated in a much more decorative way – for example, creams and jellies were often moulded into fancy shapes and fish and poultry were presented elaborately garnished.

During the Victorian era the settings became more ornate, with underplates to the dinner plates, saucers to the cups and silver or crystal cruets rowed along the table. And by the end of the 19th century, elaborate centrepieces came into vogue. These were invariably based around multi-tiered silver or glass stands that held displays of fruit or flowers.

At Christmas breakfast (*above centre*), lunch (*left*) and tea (*above right*), we make a point of using china, cutlery and glassware in traditional designs. Many Victorian china patterns, and even a few 18th-century ones, are still made today by their original manufacturers. Search out services by companies like Royal Worcester, Crown Derby and Wedgwood, Herend and Limoges. Traditional cutlery patterns such as King's and Old English are also still manufactured, either in silver, silver-plate or contemporary stainless steel. Glassware, too, can be found in period designs – look especially for Waterford crystal, the Victorian's favourite.

FRUIT CONE

A fruit cone makes a dramatic centre-piece for a festive table. Our version includes fresh flowers, plums and grapes. If you substitute dried flowers and fruit the display will last even longer, and as an alternative to making the moss base yourself you can buy one ready-made from a florist or garden centre.

MATERIALS

Sphagnum moss cone (or wire frame, chicken wire and moss to make your own); fine- and medium-gauge florist's stub wire; wire cutters; scissors; glue gun; walnuts; grapes; kumquats; dates; ivy berries; box greenery; roses ('Vicky Brown'); spurge; Chinese lanterns; black plums; pine cones; apples; holly and berries.

1 Fill the frame with damp sphagnum moss, securing in place with chicken wire. If necessary, pack with extra moss by poking it through the holes in the wire.

2 Pierce the base of each walnut with medium-gauge stub wire and secure with a blob of glue. Trim the wire so it won't emerge from the other side when inserted into the cone. Pierce the bottom of each grape, date and kumquat with fine-gauge wire and trim to length. Push the wire of the top walnut straight down into the cone. Attach other nuts and fruits by bending their wires at right-angles to their bases before inserting them.

3 Twist fine-gauge wire around the stems of the ivy berries and push diagonally into the moss. Attach the box greenery by making two "hairpins" out of medium-

gauge wire and pressing them over the stems and into the moss at a diagonal. Secure the roses as the ivy berries.

4 Attach the spurge as the box, but take care when trimming stems as they exude liquid that irritates the skin.

5 Continue down the cone, adding Chinese lanterns, plums, pine cones, apples and additional nuts, box and ivy berries. Push the stems of the lanterns directly into the moss. Wire each pine cone by looping medium-gauge wire around the base and twisting the ends together. Wire the bottom of each apple by inserting two medium-gauge wires at right-angles to each other, twisting the ends together underneath, and push in at right-angles.

6 Fill gaps between the apples with wired holly, holly berries and ivy berries.

VICTORIAN-STYLE CRACKER

Using coloured papers, felts, ribbons and trims, Victorian-style crackers, like the ones Tasha made *opposite*, can be made using the basic technique shown here.

MATERIALS

Craft knife; scissors; ruler; flexible white card; double-sided adhesive tape; gold thread; gold foil; mottoes and novelties; red paper-backed felt; red pleated organza ribbon; purple wire-edged pleated shot silk; gold cord; glue; jewelled fashion trimming.

1 Using a craft knife, cut three rectangles from flexible white card. The largest, the middle section, measures 15cm/6in by

21cm/8¹⁄₃in. The outer sections both measure 10cm/4in by 21cm/8¹⁄₃in. Roll the rectangles into tubes, slightly overlapping the edges by equal amounts. Secure with adhesive tape and remove backing.

2 Butt-joint the two shorter tubes to either side of the longer middle tube. Secure with adhesive tape and remove backing. Cover one of the two joins with 4cm/1¹⁄₂in wide strips of gold foil. Wind a

length of gold thread around the centre of the foil, pull to crimp and compress the tube, tie securely and cut off loose ends. Drop mottoes and novelties into the middle tube. Wrap foil and thread around the other join. Fix 2¹⁄₂cm/1in wide strips of double-sided tape around both ends of the assembled tube, remove backing and cover with foil cut to the same width.

3 Cut three rectangles of red paper-backed felt. Their lengths equal the circumference of the tubes – approx. 20¹⁄₂cm/8in. The width of the one that covers the middle tube is 13¹⁄₂cm/5¹⁄₄in. The width of the other two is 9cm/3¹⁄₂in. Then wrap each piece of felt around its tube, securing to the adhesive tape.

4 Wrap lengths of red, pleated organza ribbon over the gold foil and around the joins. Repeat with narrower lengths of purple, wire-edged, pleated shot silk. Secure in place with gold cord and, finally, glue on a jewelled fashion trimming.

CANDLES AND FLOWERS

Candles always lend a festive glow to any flower arrangement. I find a small display in a simple pot or bowl looks particularly effective on a side table or a windowsill, but a pair works equally well at either end of a larger table.

MATERIALS

Terracotta pot; plastic sheeting; dry foam block; sphagnum moss; florist's tape; scissors; medium-gauge florist's stub wire; glue gun; beeswax candles; grape ivy; blue pine; eucalyptus; anemones; white Singapore orchids; gold-sprayed poppy seedheads; chestnuts.

1 Line the terracotta pot with plastic sheeting. Cut the dry foam block to size, soak in water and place in the pot. Having packed out the sides with sphagnum moss, secure the top with florist's tape. Then tape two stub wires to the base of each candle and push into the foam.

2 Trim the stems of the grape ivy, blue pine and eucalyptus and, working from out to in, push securely into the foam (to a minimum depth of 1¼cm/½in) around the base of the candles. As an alternative to the foliage shown here you could, if you wish, use yew, laurel or bay.

3 Trim the stems of the anemones, white Singapore orchids and gold-sprayed poppy seedheads and insert through the foliage and securely into the foam. Suitable alternative flowers include Christmas roses and freesias.

4 As a finishing touch, push lengths of stub wire into the bases of some chestnuts, securing with blobs of glue (*see* page 41) and insert into the foam and among the flowers and foliage.

FOOD & DRINK

For centuries most northern cultures have had a major celebration around the time of the shortest day of the year – 21st December. Predating the essentially Christian festival we know today, the Vikings worshipped Odin and the ancient Romans celebrated Saturnalia to placate the gods and ensure a return of the sun and an end to the bleak mid-winter. There was certainly a need for a good feast and drink at this often miserable time of year; the consumption of large quantities of food, wine and ale in the company of one's fellow man fortifying against the cold, warming the heart and cheering the soul.

In Britain the Christian festival gradually took over from the Druid celebrations. However, during the 17th century the Puritans took a dim view of the Feast of the Nativity. In 1644 they declared it unlawful and issued an edict to say that all should fast on this holy day. Troops were mustered to ensure that no one cooked lunch, and during the 12-year ban – lifted with the restoration of the monarchy – many prosecutions were brought.

The return of the English royalists from Europe led to a wider appreciation of drink in general and wine in particular, and by the 18th century the choice of foods and wines available increased as the English established themselves as one of the great trading nations of the world. In *Read's Weekly Journal* of 9th January, 1731, Mr Thomas North describes his Christmas entertainment in a merchant's house in London thus:

" . . . turkies, geese, capons, puddings of a dozen sorts more than I have ever seen in my life, besides brawn, roast beef and many things of which I know not the names, minc'd pies in abundance and a thing they call plumb pottage".

A boar's head had traditionally occupied pride of place on the table, but beef, goose and turkey were also eaten. (The turkey arrived in England in the 16th century, having been discovered in South America. However, it only became popular during the latter half of the 19th century – Mrs Beeton thought it "one of the most glorious presents made by the New World to the Old".)

In the early 19th century it was customary for Christmas dinner to be taken at 4pm, as it had been during the 18th century, but as the century progressed some people ate at 1.30pm, while others put the meal back to 8pm, the decision usually being based on whether you had children or not and whether they shared the main feast.

Many of the traditions we associate with our modern festival were introduced by the Victorians. One of the most universal expectations of the Victorian Christmas was a good feast, and perhaps one of the surprises is the variety and quantity of dishes served. Dickens wrote at great length about how important the traditional Christmas fare was to even a modest Victorian household: the Cratchits, as well as their goose, enjoyed "a pudding, like

Right: A light fruit punch (for recipe, see page 142) is always well received by guests at our Boxing Day buffet.

a speckled cannonball, so hard and firm, blazing in ignited brandy with holly stuck onto the top". The origin of the Christmas pudding is the medieval plum porridge or pottage – a leftover dish filled with meat, breadcrumbs, raisins, spices, currants, prunes and red wine, and the forerunner of mincemeat.

Traditional fare was roast beef in the North and goose in the South. While many landowners slaughtered an animal to give their workers a piece of beef for Christmas, the working classes in the cities joined "Goose Clubs", paying in a perecentage of their weekly wage

derived from the Anglo-Saxon "waes hael", which meant "Be in Health", or "Here's to You", was a mixture of mulled ale, eggs, curdled cream, roasted apples, nuts and spices.)

Of course, many of the Victorian traditions originated with the Royal Family. For example, mince pies appeared on the Royal Christmas Day menus not long after Victoria came to the throne, and rapidly overtook plum pudding in popularity among the rest of the population. A royal Christmas repast was certainly quite exotic. In 1840 at Windsor Castle, Queen Victoria hosted dinner for 18. The meal started with turtle soup, sole, and then a choice of roast

Left: *Presented in a cut-glass bowl, caramelized fruits make a luxurious edible gift. (For recipe, see page 146.)*

Above left: *"Dogs helping themselves to the pudding" by S.E. Walker (1879).*
Middle: *"The boar's head" by John Gilbert*

(from the London Illustrated News of 1855).
Right: *"Stirring the pudding" by Henry Woods (1881).*

throughout the year, usually to the local publican. Upon receiving the goose, they would take it to the baker for cooking on Christmas Day. The middle classes, on the other hand, fared better, usually enjoying a feast of turkey, beef, boiled leg of mutton and oysters.

In addition to wine, the Victorians also enjoyed port jelly, hot toddy, mulled wine, punch and wassail. (The latter,

swan or beef. Next, chicken, turbot, partridge, curried rabbit was followed by capon, pheasant, or veal. Mince pies were followed by the traditional Christmas pudding and finally a savoury. If that wasn't enough, on the side-tables there was turkey pie, partridge, boar's head, sausages, brawn, roast beef, pork, roast mutton and roast turkey. Today, our Christmas food looks quite plain in comparison!

CHRISTMAS EVE SUPPER

Christmas Eve supper is a meal we share with relatives and close friends. I serve informal, comforting food suitable for a cold night, rather than setting out to impress with lots of small, intricate courses, and to avoid any last minute panics prepare most of it in advance.

Guests are welcomed with a glass or two of mulled wine and a selection of hot pastry nibbles, including spicy sausage and vegetarian rolls, puff pastry straws and Marmite pinwheels, all of which can be cooked from frozen in a few minutes.

At the table I invariably offer a light soup to start with, such as vegetable consommé with basil, followed by a huge fish pie topped with mashed potato and served with green peas with bacon and baby onion rings. My favourite white Burgundy – Puligny-Montrachet (1985) Domaine Leflaive – is a wonderful accompaniment to the fish pie, and Martin usually provides a Bordeaux, such as a St Julien Château Gloria (1982).

For those who feel hungry on returning from Midnight Mass, I offer a light snack – usually hot and fruity prunes and apricots wrapped in bacon, traditional hot mince pies and creamy egg nog.

MULLED WINE

3 bottles full-bodied red wine
2 cinnamon sticks, halved
12 cloves
½ teaspoon Angostura bitters
80g/3oz caster sugar
Enough for 20 glasses

Mix the ingredients together and heat slowly in a stainless steel saucepan. Do not let the mixture boil as this would spoil the flavour. Serve in small glasses or small china mugs.

SPICY SAUSAGE ROLLS

500g/1lb puff pastry
Spicy sausage meat:
500g/1lb pork sausage meat
1 teaspoon cayenne pepper
3 cloves of garlic, crushed
1 tablespoon of spicy mustard
1 tablespoon Worcester Sauce
1 teaspoon Tabasco
Makes about 40 small sausage rolls

To make the meat, mix all the ingredients together and refrigerate until required.

Roll the pastry out into a rectangle 25cm/10in by 37½cm/15in, then cut three strips 7½cm/3in wide. Divide the sausage meat into three and roll each third into a long sausage. Lay a sausage on each of the 3 strips, roll the pastry over the sausage and seal the edges with cold water by pressing together.

Cut the rolls into 2½cm/1in pieces and bake in a preheated oven at 200°C/400°F/Gas Mark 6, till puffed and golden.

VEGETARIAN ROLLS

500g/1lb mushrooms
2 large onions, very finely chopped
4 tablespoons olive oil
2 large cloves garlic
2 teaspoons curry powder
1 teaspoon ground turmeric
125g/4oz fine fresh breadcrumbs
3 tablespoons chopped parsley
2 eggs
Makes 20 rolls

Chop the mushrooms finely. Cook the onions in oil over medium heat until soft. Add spices and cook for 2 minutes, stirring continuously. Add breadcrumbs and chopped parsley and remove from heat. Allow to cool a little, then stir in the eggs. Allow to cool before rolling into a sausage. Continue as for sausage rolls (*see* left), using half the quantity of pastry.

MARMITE PINWHEELS

250g/8oz puff pastry
Marmite
Makes approximately 40 pinwheels

Roll the puff pastry into a 25cm/10in square. Brush thinly with Marmite, then roll into a tight sausage. Slice into thick discs about ½cm/¼in thick. Lay flat on a baking sheet and bake until they are crisp and golden.

PUFF PASTRY STRAWS

500g/1lb puff pastry, defrosted
Grated Parmesan cheese, Marmite or ground paprika for sprinkling over the straws
Makes approximately 40 straws

Cut the pastry in half and roll each half into a 25cm/10in square. Cut into long

strips 1¼cm/½in wide, then cut in half to make about 40 straws. Scatter Parmesan or ground paprika over the pastry, or spread with Marmite, then lift each strip

onto a lightly greased baking tray. Twist each strip as you place it on the tray then bake in a hot oven at 200°C/400°F/Gas Mark 6 until golden and crisp.

VEGETABLE CONSOMME WITH BASIL

3 tablespoons olive oil
2 medium onions, peeled and chopped
6 small leeks, diced and washed
4 medium carrots, peeled and diced
6 garlic cloves, peeled and sliced
8 large handfuls assorted leaves – watercress,
    young spinach, lettuce, mustard, greens,
    parsley, sorrel, etc., very finely chopped
2¼ pints vegetable stock or water
salt and pepper
4 heaped tablespoons of bottled pesto
sauce (or to taste)
Serves 10

Cook the onions, leeks, carrots and garlic in the olive oil over a gentle heat until soft, stirring occasionally. Add the leaves and continue to cook till they have wilted. Add the stock and simmer gently for about 25 minutes. Season with salt, pepper and pesto sauce. Serve the soup hot with a leaf or two of watercress or parsley in the centre and, if you wish, a cheese straw to the side.

FISH PIE

2kg/4¹/₂lb smoked haddock and cod
190ml/¹/₃ pint milk
150g/6oz butter
150g/6oz flour
350g/12oz peeled prawns
350g/12oz button mushrooms
6 tablespoons chopped parsley
salt, pepper and lemon juice
2.7kg/6lb boiled potatoes, mashed with
*   125g/4oz butter, 250ml/8fl oz milk, and*
*   seasoned with salt and pepper.*
Serves 12

Bake the fish with milk in a shallow dish in a preheated oven at 400°F/200°C/ Gas Mark 6 for 20 minutes, or until the fish comes away from the bones. Melt the butter in a saucepan and stir in flour. Cook over a moderate heat to form a roux, pour in the cooking liquid from the fish, stir till smooth then simmer gently on low heat for 15 minutes.

Remove the fish from the skin and bones and fold into the sauce with the prawns, mushrooms and parsley. Season with salt, pepper and lemon juice. Spoon into a pie dish and cover with mashed potatoes, forking the top. Bake for 30 minutes till golden brown.

GREEN PEAS, BACON AND BABY ONIONS

1¹/₂kg/3lb fresh shelled or frozen peas
50g/2oz butter
125g/4oz tiny onions, peeled
1 large sprig of thyme
125g/4oz bacon, cubed
salt and pepper
Serves 12

Put peas and butter in a casserole dish, add other ingredients and simmer, covered, for 25 minutes and season.

APRICOTS AND PRUNES IN BACON

12 rashers of streaky bacon
12 stoned prunes, soaked until plump
12 stoned dried apricots, soaked until plump
Makes 24

Remove rinds from the bacon. Lay the rashers on a chopping board and stretch by rubbing with the flat of a knife.

Stuff the apricots with the prunes and roll in a rasher of bacon. Secure with a cocktail stick. Cook under a hot grill and serve piping hot.

EGG NOG

12 eggs, separated
350g/12oz sugar
300ml/10fl oz bourbon, brandy or sherry
125ml/4fl oz rum
250ml/¹/₂ pint double cream
grated nutmeg
Serves 12

Whisk the egg yolks with the sugar until pale and creamy, add the bourbon and rum and then pour in the cream.

Whisk the egg whites until stiff, then fold into the yolks and cream. Pour into glasses and serve with grated nutmeg.

MINCE PIES

375g/12oz puff pastry
500g/1lb mincemeat
milk or egg to glaze
icing sugar
Makes approximately 20 pies

Roll out the pastry to a thickness of approximately 3mm/⅛in. Stamp out 20 or so rounds with a 7½cm/3in cookie cutter, and an equal amount with a 6¼cm/2½in cutter for the tops.

Line shallow patty tins with the larger discs of pastry. Divide the mincemeat between them, then brush the edges lightly with milk or beaten egg. Press the tops down, sealing the edges firmly. Brush with more beaten egg or milk and bake in a hot oven, preheated to 220°C/425°F/Gas Mark 7, until golden and well risen. Remove from the tins to a cooling rack and dust with icing sugar.

CHRISTMAS DAY BREAKFAST

With the children up and about early and impatient to open some of their presents, I make sure Christmas Day breakfast is easy to prepare and doesn't go on for too long. Stuffed papaya served with Perrier-Jouet champagne provides a sparkling start to the morning. Potato pancakes with crème fraîche and bacon are always a great success, and I never seem to make enough. A Christmas muesli, made by adding apricots, prunes, dried tropical fruits and brazil nuts to a bought muesli, and served with yoghurt or milk, is especially popular with our three vegetarian daughters. To satisfy large appetites and a sweet tooth, marmalade muffins, served with coffee, round off the meal.

STUFFED PAPAYA

4 large, ripe papayas
1 baby pineapple
1 small mango
Champagne
Serves 4

Cut the papaya in half and scoop out the seeds with a teaspoon. Scoop the flesh from 4 of the halves with a melon-baller. Peel and chop the pineapple and place in a bowl with the papaya flesh. Peel the mango and cut the flesh from the stone, without losing any of the juice. Add to the other fruits.

Place the remaining halves of papaya on plates. Fill with the tropical fruits, scattering any extra on the plates. Pour the juices from the bottom of the bowl into the papaya. When everyone is at the table, open the Champagne and pour a little into each papaya so that it mixes with the juice and froths up.

POTATO PANCAKES WITH CREME FRAICHE AND BACON

1kg/2lb potatoes, peeled
1 medium onion
5 tablespoons flour
2 eggs, beaten
salt and pepper
oil for frying
crème fraîche
rashers of streaky bacon
Serves 4-6

Grate the potatoes and the onion. Place in a colander and squeeze dry. Mix with the rest of the ingredients.

Heat 1¼cm/½in of oil in a shallow pan. Drop two tablespoons of the mixture into the oil and smooth with the back of a spoon to form a small pancake. Fry until golden, then turn to cook the other side.

Continue until all the mixture is used up, cooking 4 pancakes at a time. Remove the pancakes with a palette knife and drain on kitchen paper. Then place on a warm platter and top with crème fraîche and a crisp half-rasher of bacon.

MARMALADE MUFFINS

250g/8oz plain flour
1 tablespoon baking powder
75g/3oz caster sugar
pinch of salt
1 egg
250ml/8fl oz milk
50g/2oz softened butter
5 tablespoons marmalade
Makes 12 muffins

Mix the flour, baking powder, sugar and salt together. Beat the egg and milk in a bowl, then beat in the softened butter. Add the liquid to the dry ingredients, and stir briefly to mix. If the batter is lumpy, don't worry.

Butter 12 deep bun tins. Spoon 2 tablespoons of batter into each one, followed by a teaspoonful of marmalade. Add the remaining batter. Bake in a preheated oven for about 18 minutes at 200°C/400°F/Gas Mark 6 until risen and golden.

CHRISTMAS DAY LUNCH

Before sitting down to Christmas lunch at about 1.30 we have a few friends and neighbours around at midday for a glass of champagne – either Perrier-Jouet or, as a special treat, Krug Grande Cuvée. With last minute preparations for the meal continuing throughout it, this is a very informal and jolly affair.

the two, and prepare the latter with bulgar wheat and pecans. It is worth remembering that fresh goose, a truly seasonal bird, is only available after Michaelmas, so you will have to buy frozen. Also, geese are longer and flatter than turkeys – a 6.5kg/14lb bird is the maximum for a domestic oven.

For the vegetarians in the family I make a chestnut roast, served with a deli-

Excellent white wines to accompany the meal are a Rully "La Fontaine" (1985) Louis Jadot, or a Saint Aubin (1986) Louis Jadot. For a rounded and well-balanced red, the Pomerol (1986) Château Graves Guillot is a fine choice.

Christmas pudding can be made one year in advance for the next, although in truth it actually tastes no different to a freshly made one. It is only the colour

We always start the lunch with a soup, such as Stilton with red cabbage and juniper. This is very rich and best served in small cups on a saucer and eaten with a teaspoon. For the best flavour choose a very ripe Stilton.

While turkey has been the traditional Christmas bird in many countries since the 17th century, goose is the preferred alternative throughout Germany and Eastern Europe. We alternate between

cious Cumberland sauce – although a simple tomato sauce can be just as nice an accompaniment.

Whether you serve chestnut roast, goose or turkey, roast potatoes are an essential part of the Christmas meal. I usually serve sweet potatoes as well, together with sprouts and chestnuts. (There's no need to spend time peeling fresh chestnuts as tinned or dried ones will do just as well.)

which becomes darker. I invariably gild the pudding for effect and, in accordance with tradition, stuff it with charms and coins, which can be handed back by the lucky recipients and saved from year to year. Brandy butter is a traditional accompaniment to the pudding.

For those who prefer something more refreshing, I make a Christmas pudding bombe – a rich ice-cream with the distinct flavour of traditional Christmas pudding.

STILTON SOUP WITH RED CABBAGE AND JUNIPER

75g/3oz butter
50g/2oz flour
1 litre/2 pints hot chicken stock
250ml/8 fl oz double cream
250ml/8 fl oz white wine
500g/1lb Stilton cheese (very ripe), crumbled
250g/8oz red cabbage, shredded finely
1 tablespoon groundnut oil
1 teaspoon juniper berries
salt and freshly ground pepper
Makes 10 small cups

Melt the butter in a heavy-based saucepan, tip in the flour and stir for 4 or 5 minutes. Pour in the stock and beat with a whisk or wooden spoon until the mixture thickens. Pour in the cream and then the wine. Bring the mixture up to the boil then turn down to a simmer.

Add the crumbled Stilton, stirring continuously. Season with a little salt if necessary and some black pepper. Heat the oil in a shallow pan, add the cabbage and the juniper and stir-fry for 2 or 3 minutes until the cabbage is slightly softened. Season with black pepper. Divide the cabbage equally between warm cups or soup plates, then spoon the hot soup around each pile of cabbage.

ROAST GOOSE WITH BULGAR WHEAT AND PECANS

To calculate the cooking time for a goose multiply the weight in pounds by 25 minutes – i.e. a 6kg/13lb goose will take approximately 5½ hours.

1 goose, about 5½-7kg/12-16lb in weight
Stuffing:
8 stalks of celery
250g/8oz bulgar wheat
250g/8oz white breadcrumbs
salt and black pepper
3 eggs, beaten
50g/2oz butter, melted
125g/4oz shelled pecan nuts
grated zest of 1 large orange
Serves 6-10

Chop the celery finely and mix with the other ingredients to make the stuffing. Place the bird in a large roasting tin, pull away any surplus fat from the inside of the bird and prick it all over with a skewer. Roast for 20 minutes at 200°C/400°F/Gas Mark 6.

Remove the bird from the oven and fill it with most of the stuffing. Turn the oven down to 180°C/350°F/Gas Mark 4, then return the goose to the oven until cooked. While the goose is cooking make stock with the giblets. Simmer the giblets with enough water to cover, an onion and a bay leaf for 40 minutes.

When the bird is cooked transfer it to a large warm platter, keeping it warm in the switched-off oven. Pour the pan juices into a jug and leave to settle. The fat will float to the top leaving a residue of meat juices underneath. Pour off the fat. Place the roasting tin over a low heat and pour in the juices and the stock, seasoning to taste with salt and pepper. Allow to reduce slightly, then pour into a warm jug and serve with the bird.

As a garnish for the goose you can serve stuffed oranges. Slice the tops off as many small oranges as you have guests and scoop out the flesh. Chop it and mix with the remaining stuffing. Pile back into the shells and place in the oven, brushing with a little butter or oil 10–15 minutes before the bird is cooked.

ROAST TURKEY

A 3.5kg/8lb bird will feed 10 people. A 9kg/20lb bird will comfortably feed almost 30 people but may be uncomfortably large to handle. Remember that just under half of the weight is made up of bones, but some people will only want small portions, particularly if there are elderly family members eating. It is best, however, not to underestimate the appetites of children.

To calculate the cooking time of a turkey multiply the weight in pounds by 20 minutes, then add 20 minutes. Allow a further 20 minutes standing time to make the bird easier to carve.

1 turkey, about 7kg/15lb in weight
Chestnut, celery and sausage meat stuffing
salt
150g/5oz softened butter or dripping
175g/6oz fat bacon rashers

Rinse the inside of the turkey with cold water and pat dry with kitchen paper. Stuff the neck cavity with your choice of stuffing, putting any remaining in the body end. Rub the skin of the bird with salt and smear with the butter or dripping. Cover the breast of the bird with the bacon rashers and wrap the legs with two layers of foil to prevent them drying out.

Cover the entire bird with kitchen foil

and place in a large roasting tin. Set the bird in a preheated low oven on a low shelf at 170°C/325°F/Gas Mark 3. For the last hour of cooking turn the heat up to 200°C/400°C/Gas Mark 6, remove the foil and the bacon from the breast and allow the bird to brown. It will need about 5 hours in total, but oven temperatures vary considerably so it is best that you test the bird after 4 hours or so to see if it is done. The most accurate way to do this is to pierce the leg or breast with a skewer; the juices that run out should be clear without any trace of pink, which would indicate the bird is not done yet. If the juices run clear then the turkey is ready.

Remove from the oven and allow to rest for 20 minutes or so before carving. Meanwhile make the gravy. Lift the tin so that all the fat and juices run to one corner. Spoon off as much of the fat as you can without disturbing the dark juices underneath. Set the pan over a low heat, work in a couple of tablespoons of flour and whisk in enough stock to form a pourable gravy. Allow it to bubble gently for a few minutes to give a concentrated flavour, then season with salt and pepper and pour into a warm gravy boat or jug.

(An alternative method of cooking turkey is to fill it with fat and cook in a very hot oven for a couple of hours.)

Serve the turkey with bacon rolls and chipolata sausages cooked under the grill while everything else is in the oven.

Bread sauce is a traditional accompaniment, although many people choose not to serve it nowadays. A quick and easy way to make it is to put day-old bread, a little chopped onion, milk, butter and ground

cloves into the liquidizer, whizz, then heat gently in a small saucepan until thick.

CHESTNUT, CELERY AND SAUSAGE MEAT STUFFING

500g/1lb tinned chestnuts
1 stick of celery, finely chopped
1 large onion, peeled and chopped
250g/8oz sausage meat
30g/1oz butter
85g/3oz breadcrumbs
500ml/1 pint chicken stock
salt
pepper
Makes enough for 7kg/15lb bird

Chop the chestnuts and mix with the celery and chicken stock. Boil until tender, then drain. Cook the onions in the butter, then leave to cool. Mix the breadcrumbs and sausage meat. Season well and, finally, mix all the ingredients together.

ROAST POTATOES

The way to ensure roast potatoes are crisp is to pre-cook them in boiling water before roasting. Cut them into similar sizes, drop into boiling salted water and cook for 10 minutes over a medium heat. Drain, and cook in dripping in a heavy roasting dish near the top of the oven until golden and crisp. Shake occasionally to ensure they crisp on all sides. It may sound over-generous but allow 6 potatoes per person.

SPROUTS AND CHESTNUTS

Brussels sprouts are the traditional

accompaniment to Christmas turkey, and are often mixed with chestnuts. Allow 500g/1lb chestnuts and 1½kg/3lb sprouts for 10 people. Tinned chestnuts work well if you heat them gently in plenty of stock, then mix into the cooked sprouts. Soak dried chestnuts overnight, then cook in stock for 25 minutes or until tender.

CHESTNUT ROAST

250g/8oz hazelnuts
250g/8oz tinned chestnuts, drained or
*   reconstituted dried chestnuts*
4 medium onions, peeled and chopped
2 tablespoons groundnut oil
500g/8oz tomatoes, chopped and seeded
1 small hot chilli, seeded and finely chopped
2 cloves of garlic, peeled and thinly sliced
175g/6oz fresh breadcrumbs
2 tablespoons chopped mixed herbs
3 tablespoons chopped fresh parsley
2 eggs, beaten
salt and freshly ground black pepper
Serves 6

Chop the nuts finely. Sauté the onion in oil till soft and golden. Stir in tomatoes, chilli and garlic and continue cooking over medium heat for 5-6 minutes until some of the liquid has evaporated.

Grease and line a 1kg/2lb loaf tin. Remove the tomato mixture from the heat and stir in breadcrumbs, chopped nuts, herbs and eggs. Season with salt and pepper and pack into the prepared loaf tin. Bake for 35-40 minutes in a preheated oven at 220°C/425°F/Gas Mark 7. Remove and set aside for 5 minutes before turning out and slicing.

1

VEGETABLE PARCELS

These vegetable parcels proved a great success with our three vegetarian daughters, Tanya (who made them), Tasha and Cara. They can be served as a starter to a main course, or as a side-dish with salmon, or as a snack. You can also adapt the basic recipe to your own ideas, adding herbs or garlic or changing the vegetables to include your favourites.

4 medium-sized carrots, scrubbed

250g/8oz broccoli florets

125g/4oz mushrooms, thinly sliced

30g/1oz butter

500g/1lb puff pastry, defrosted

salt and pepper

8 heaped tablespoons crème fraîche

4 tablespoons chopped mixed fresh herbs
*   (optional) e.g. parsley, tarragon and chervil*

1 small egg, beaten

Makes 8 parcels

1 Cut the carrots into thin matchsticks and steam them for 2 or 3 minutes until they soften slightly. Steam or blanch the broccoli until it is bright green and tender. Sauté the mushrooms in the butter until they are golden brown.

2

4

Roll out the puff pastry to form 8 squares, each measuring 15cm by 15cm/6in by 6in. Divide the vegetables evenly between the squares, piling them up in the centre of each one. Season with salt and pepper.

2 Having placed a spoonful of crème fraîche on top of the vegetables and scattered on the fresh herbs, brush around the edges of the squares of pastry with a little beaten egg.

3 Fold the four corners of each square together to form a parcel, pinching the edges firmly together to hold the filling in place. Brush each parcel with a little more

3

beaten egg and then transfer them, using a wide spatula, to a baking sheet.

Bake in a preheated oven at 200°C/400°F/Gas Mark 6 for 15-20 minutes, until crisp and golden brown.

4 Serve the parcels hot, with an additional spoonful of crème fraîche on the side if you wish.

CUMBERLAND SAUCE

Cumberland Sauce makes a good accompaniment to Chestnut Roast, but a rich tomato sauce would work well too.

2 shallots, finely chopped
1 lemon
1 orange
3 tablespoons redcurrant jelly
150ml/5 fl oz port
2 teaspoons wine vinegar
ground ginger
Serves 10

Blanch the shallots in boiling water for a minute or two, then drain. Thinly pare the rind of the fruit and cut into fine shreds. Blanch in boiling water for 1 minute, then drain. Squeeze the juice from the fruit.

Melt the redcurrant jelly in a small heavy-based saucepan. Add the shallots, citrus rind, fruit juice, port, vinegar and a pinch of ground ginger. Bring to the boil, remove from the heat and serve either warm or cold.

GILDED CHRISTMAS PUDDING

If you prefer to make a traditional pudding shape then put the mixture into 2 x 1½ pint basins, well buttered and covered with greaseproof paper and muslin.

500g/1lb seedless raisins
150g/6oz candied orange and lemon peel, finely
    chopped
150g/6oz glacé cherries
75g/3oz almonds, blanched and chopped

250g/8oz melted butter
250g/8oz fresh breadcrumbs
3 eggs, beaten
100ml/3½fl oz stout
4 tablespoons brandy or whisky
Serves 12

Mix all the ingredients together. Put the mixture into a large, good quality freezer bag. Seal the bag with string, leaving plenty of space for the pudding to expand. Roll the mixture gently to achieve a cannonball shape. Wrap the pudding in muslin and tie a knot at the top, securing

a wooden spoon in the knot as you do so to hang the pudding from.

Place the pudding in a large deep pan so that it is supported by the spoon and does not touch the bottom of the pan. Put enough boiling water in the pan to come half way up the hanging pudding. Cover as best you can with the lid and wrap a dome of tin foil over the lid to seal in as much of the steam as possible. Simmer for 8 hours or until the pudding is cooked, topping up the water every hour or so. Take care when lifting the foil as the steam that escapes is very hot.

Leave to rest for 30 minutes before removing from the water and unwrapping onto a serving dish.

To gild the pudding

Remove a sheet of gold leaf from its book together with the protective paper backing. (Booklets of gold transfer leaf are readily available from craft shops and artist's suppliers.) You must handle the sheet carefully so that the gold leaf does not break up and come off on your fingers.

Place the sheet over the pudding with the gold leaf side facing downwards and gently rub over the protective paper backing either with your finger tips or the rounded end of a knife handle as if you were applying a transfer.

Carefully peel away the backing sheet, leaving the gold leaf stuck to the surface of the pudding.

Repeat the process with additional sheets of gold transfer leaf until you have completed the gilding process. (You will need approximately 6 sheets of gold transfer leaf to cover approximately the top third of the pudding.)

CHRISTMAS PUDDING ICE CREAM

6 eggs
175g/6oz caster sugar
250g/8oz leftover Christmas pudding
3 tablespoons brandy
375g/12oz double cream
Serves 6

Separate the eggs. Whisk the yolks with the sugar until light and fluffy. Break up the Christmas pudding into large crumbs and fold into the eggs and sugar. Beat the cream to soft peaks then fold into the mixture. Beat the egg whites till stiff and gently mix in with the brandy.

Pour the mixture into a bombe mould and freeze for 6 hours or until set. (*Note:* This ice-cream does not set very hard.) Serve in small portions, preferably with a glass of sweet wine, such as Château Coutet (1971).

BRANDY BUTTER

350g/12oz unsalted butter, at room
*   temperature*
250g/8oz caster sugar
juice and grated rind of 1 orange
brandy to taste
Serves 12

Soften the butter and beat with the sugar until light and fluffy. Use an electric whisk if you have one. Stir in the orange rind. Gradually add the orange juice and brandy, tasting as you go. Stop before the mixture curdles.

Chill in the fridge for at least an hour before serving.

CHRISTMAS DAY HIGH TEA

To be honest, we usually eat so much at Christmas lunch that come late teatime nobody can face any more food. However, it has been known for me to rustle up an informal high tea and serve it round the fire about 7 pm.

Welsh rarebit (made with Stilton) and a Kitchen Garden salad is easy to prepare and can be followed by a Scots Black Bun or a traditional cut-and-come-again fruit bread. A thin, crisp shortbread can also be offered, along with Christmas cake, which can of course be eaten at any time up to Twelfth Night.

STILTON RAREBIT WITH KITCHEN GARDEN SALAD

250g/8oz Stilton cheese
30g/1oz butter, softened
1 tablespoon Worcestershire sauce
1 tablespoon English mustard
2 tablespoons beer
4 slices of toast
Serves 4

Grate the cheese and mix to a paste with the other ingredients. Spread the mixture over toast and grill until bubbling. Cut each slice into four and serve with salad.

To make the salad with mustard dressing, dress handfuls of leaves, white and red chicory, oak leaf lettuce and batavia with mustardy vinaigrette. Blend 6 parts extra virgin olive oil with 2 parts white wine vinegar and 1 part grainy mustard. Season with salt and pepper and toss the leaves gently in the dressing.

FRUIT BREAD

500g/1lb strong plain flour
1 tablespoon fast-acting dried yeast
125g/4oz currants
75g/3oz sultanas
75g/3oz raisins
125g/4oz butter, diced
75g/3oz light brown sugar
100ml/3¹/₂fl oz warm milk
¹/₄ teaspoon mixed spice
¹/₄ teaspoon cinnamon
1 large egg, well beaten
1 tablespoon molasses
Serves 10

Put the flour into a large mixing bowl and rub in the butter with your fingertips. Mix the yeast with the milk and a large pinch of the sugar. Add the remaining ingredients to the flour. Leave the yeast in a warm place for 5 or 10 minutes until frothy, then pour it into the bowl containing the flour and fruit.

Pour the beaten egg into the mixture and mix the whole lot to a soft dough, adding a little water if the dough is too stiff or a little flour if it is too wet.

Melt the molasses in a small pan over a medium heat and stir in the water. Pour in the dough and knead thoroughly. Cover the bowl with a cloth and leave in a warm place for about an hour until risen to twice the original volume.

Turn the dough out into a generously buttered 1kg/2lb loaf tin. Return to the warm place for a further 30 minutes. Bake the loaf in a preheated oven at 180°C/350°F/Gas Mark 4 for 1 to 1¾ hours. The loaf is cooked when it sounds hollow.

BLACK BUN

1kg/2lb plain flour
25g/1oz/1 tablespoon dried yeast
450ml/15fl oz warm water
1 teaspoon salt
500g/1lb raisins
750g/1½lb currants
250g/8oz lemon and orange peel, finely
  chopped
90g/3½oz flaked almonds
½ teaspoon ground nutmeg
1 teaspoon ground ginger
1 teaspoon ground allspice
1 tablespoon brandy
1 egg, beaten
Serves 12

Sieve the flour. Dissolve the yeast in the water, then mix with the flour and the salt

to form a dough. Turn onto a floured board and knead for 10 minutes until smooth and elastic. Place in a china or glass bowl in a warm place for about an hour to an hour and a half until it has doubled its size.

Put the dough on a floured board and set one third of it aside. Flatten the larger of the two pieces to a round about 2½cm/1 in thick. Mix the fruit and spices

together with the brandy and knead them into the large piece of dough. When the fruit is fully distributed throughout the dough, roll out the remaining piece 1½cm/½in thick, then place the fruited dough in the centre. Wrap the plain dough around and seal the edges underneath.

CHRISTMAS CAKE

625g/1lb 4oz currants
500g/1lb raisins
125g/4oz mixed peel, finely chopped
6 tablespoons brandy
275g/9oz plain flour
pinch salt
1 teaspoon mixed spice
300g/10oz soft brown sugar
300g/10oz unsalted butter
5 eggs, beaten lightly
1 heaped tablespoon black treacle
grated rind of 1 lemon and 1 orange
Serves 20

Soak the dried fruit overnight in the brandy.

Sieve the flour with the salt and spice. Cream the butter and sugar together until light and fluffy, then add the eggs, a little at a time. Gently fold in the spiced flour and then the soaked fruit. Stir in the

treacle and grated rind. Spoon the mixture into a 22½cm/9in cake tin lined with butter and bake in a preheated oven at 140°C/275°F/Gas Mark 1 for 4½ hours. Insert the point of a knitting needle or skewer to check if the cake is done. If it comes out clean the cake is ready.

Cool thoroughly before turning out, wrap in foil and store in a tin until ready to ice.

While the cake is in storage you may like to add a little more brandy. Turn the cake upside down and poke holes in the

bottom with a skewer or knitting needle. Spoon in a few tablespoons of brandy and wrap up with foil. You can do this every week or so until you are ready to decorate the cake.

Decorating the cake:

1kg/2lb almond paste
apricot jam

Royal icing:

750g/1½lb icing sugar

4 egg whites

1 teaspoon glycerine

A week before decorating the cake, cover it with almond paste. Dust the work surface with icing sugar. Use half the paste to roll a long thin rectangle to wrap round the sides of the cake – do this in two halves. Brush the sides of the cake with apricot jam, then press the paste on the sides, smoothing the join with a palette knife.

Roll the remaining half of the paste slightly larger than the top of the cake. Brush the top with jam and place the paste on top. Press gently to join the top and edges, trimming where necessary.

The cake is best iced a week after the almond paste has been put on. Beat the egg whites until slightly frothy, mix in the icing sugar, beat with an electric whisk until thick and fluffy, then beat in the glycerine. The icing should stand in stiff peaks. Spread the icing over the sides and top of the cake, then fork into peaks with a blunt knife. Decorate with fir-cones, holly and ribbon.

SHORTBREAD

175g/6oz plain flour

125g/4oz butter

250g/8oz sugar

Serves 8

Knead the sugar and butter together, then work in the flour to form a soft dough. Transfer to a floured baking sheet, then push the paste gently into a round, about 20cm/8in in diameter. Prick well with a fork and mark out with a knife into 8 pieces.

Bake in a preheated oven at 150°C/300°F/ Gas Mark 2, until the shortbread is a very pale golden colour. Remove from the oven and sprinkle with caster sugar. Then leave to cool before lifting onto a plate.

BOXING DAY BREAKFAST

Having almost invariably eaten too much on Christmas Day, none of the family can face anything overly rich or heavy on Boxing Day – especially at breakfast. Kedgeree, which is quick and easy to prepare, makes a light yet comforting start and is substantial enough to fuel everyone for a long morning walk in the cold. Lightly spiced poached fruits in orange juice make a refreshing accompaniment and can be served either warm or cold according to preference.

KEDGEREE

1kg/2lb smoked haddock
500g/1lb salmon
4 sprigs of parsley
1 bay leaf
6 peppercorns
75g/3oz butter
1 medium onion, peeled and chopped
350g/12oz long grain rice
4 eggs, hard-boiled and shelled
salt and black pepper
Serves 6

Put the fish in a large saucepan and add enough water to just cover. Add the parsley, bay leaf and peppercorns and simmer over a moderate heat for about 10–12 minutes until the fish comes away from the bone.

Melt half of the butter in a saucepan and cook the onion in it until soft. Add the rice and cover with 1 litre/1½ pints of boiling water. Cover and simmer for 20 minutes, or until the rice is tender. Skin and bone the fish and break into large flakes and stir into the cooked rice. Quarter and add the hard-boiled eggs and serve in a large dish. Finally, garnish with fresh herbs if you wish.

POACHED FRUITS

6 large pears
half a lemon
orange juice to cover
2 cinnamon sticks
12 cloves
1 tablespoon whole mace (optional)
pared rind of a small orange
5 tablespoons liquid honey
Serves 6

Note: Apples – a sweet dessert variety – are also successful baked in this way. You can use a vanilla pod instead of the cinnamon if you wish.

Peel the pears with a vegetable peeler, rubbing the cut side of the lemon over them to stop them turning brown. Put them on their side in a stainless steel or enamel saucepan. Pour over enough orange juice to cover the pears, then add the spices and honey. Bring to the boil, then turn down the heat. Simmer gently until tender to the point of a knife – for about 20 minutes, depending on the ripeness of the fruit.

Remove the pears to an appropriately sized serving dish. Turn up the heat under the juices and boil them rapidly for approximately 5–6 minutes until they have thickened a little. Strain the juices through a sieve over the pears. Serve either chilled or hot.

BOXING DAY BUFFET

We invite a few close friends and neighbours over for a buffet on Boxing Day. Timing depends on how late we were for breakfast, but usually people start arriving for drinks and nibbles – a light fruit punch and anchovy palmiers are usually well received – about midday and the buffet starts around 1.30 p.m. I'm often caught out still preparing the food as the guests arrive, so they get roped in to helping with the preparations. That said, many of the dishes I serve can be prepared in advance.

A cut-and-come-again turkey chestnut pie is ideal for a buffet because it can be made in advance and it is so easy for guests to slice their own. It should be made from scratch with poached meat in stock, rather than with leftover meat, which tends to be too dry. You could use chicken instead of turkey, and the top of the pie can be decorated with pastry leaves and berries, or Happy Christmas cut-out pastry letters.

Boulangère potatoes are well suited to a buffet, as they hold up well if kept warm in a low oven until everything else is ready, and will keep their heat served on a warming tray. A red salad looks festive, while a pasta, Brie, celery and walnut salad provides vegetarians with a substantial alternative to the turkey pie.

First and foremost, Boxing Day food should be a delight to the eye as much rich food has already been consumed. Consequently, there should be little tempting things to eat, like fruits dipped in caramel and Sauternes jellies, rather than huge

portions of heavy puddings. Above all, I think it is most important not to serve anything that looks like leftovers from Christmas Day!

A cake of some sort should also be offered, either the rich fruit Christmas cake, or Panettone – the traditional Italian Christmas bread – with the top cut to form the shape of a star.

Finally, after the French wines of the previous two days, we like to provide an interesting alternative, such as a New Zealand Sauvignon Blanc from Hunters, Marlborough. As for a red wine, Côte Rôtie (1985) by E. Guigal is exceptional.

FRUIT PUNCH

2 bottles of light and fruity red wine, such as a
  Beaujolais
3 tablespoons of Grand Marnier
3 small oranges stuck with cloves
2 lemons, sliced
8 tablespoons liquid honey
2 cinnamon sticks, broken in half
Enough for 20 glasses

Put all the ingredients into a stainless steel saucepan. Bring slowly to the boil. Just before the punch reaches boiling point turn down the heat and simmer gently for 15 minutes. Serve in glasses.

ANCHOVY PALMIERS

375g/12oz puff pastry
160g/6oz anchovy fillets, rinsed and
  chopped
beaten egg
Makes 40

Roll the pastry into a rectangle approximately 15cm/6in by 25cm/10in. Spread the chopped anchovies over the pastry. Fold in the two long edges until they almost meet, press them down to seal, then brush the channel in the centre with beaten egg. Fold the dough in half so that the edges meet and press firmly to seal them. Chill the dough for 15 minutes.

Slice the pastry roll into 1¼ cm/½ in thick strips. Place the strips, with one of the cut edges downwards, on a baking sheet. Chill for 20 minutes, then bake in a preheated oven at 200°C/400°F/Gas Mark 6. Bake for 6 minutes or until golden, then turn the pastries and bake the other side for 2 or 3 minutes.

Remove the pastries with a palette knife and cool on a rack.

TURKEY AND CHESTNUT PIE

1kg/2lb turkey meat, brown and white bones
  from the turkey
1 onion, peeled
2 carrots, sliced
3 stalks of celery, roughly chopped
2 bay leaves

750g/1½lb sausage meat
280g/9oz tinned chestnuts
25g/1oz gelatine powder
salt and freshly ground pepper
For the pastry:
500g/1lb plain flour
pinch of salt
125g/4oz lard
150g/6oz butter
2 eggs
iced water
beaten egg to glaze
Serves 8-10

Cover the turkey meat, bones, vegetables and aromatics with water and bring to the boil. Turn down the heat and simmer until cooked. Lift out the meat, discard the vegetables and the bones, and reserve the stock.

To make the pastry: rub the fats into the flour and salt with your fingertips. Stir in the egg and add enough water (about 8 tablespoons) to mix to a firm dough. Bring the dough together into a ball and chill for 30 minutes.

Cut the cooked turkey meat into strips and mix with the sausage meat.

Line a 22½cm/9in diameter loose-bottomed, non-stick cake tin with two-thirds of the pastry. Fill the pastry case with the chicken strips in three layers, scattering salt and freshly ground pepper and one third of the chestnuts over each layer. Then spoon in 6 tablespoons of the reserved stock.

Roll out the remaining third of the pastry and use to cover the top of the pie, wetting the edges with water and pinching together with your fingertips to seal.

Cut a hole in the top of the pie about as big as a pound coin to pour the stock through after cooking, and decorate with any spare pastry. Brush the pie with a little beaten egg and bake in a preheated oven at 180°C/350°F/Gas Mark 4 for 1 hour 10 minutes, or until golden brown.

Pour 500ml/1 pint of the stock into a pan and bring slowly to the boil. Remove from the heat and add the gelatine, stirring until dissolved. Remove the pie from the oven, then slowly pour in as much of the stock as the pie will take – do this slowly, spoonful by spoonful.

Leave the pie to cool, then refrigerate overnight. Remove the pie from its mould and serve.

BOULANGERE POTATOES

30g/1oz butter
500g/1lb medium onions, finely sliced
1kg/2lb potatoes, peeled and sliced into thin
   rounds
250ml/8fl oz chicken stock
250ml/8fl oz white wine
1 tablespoon dried thyme leaves
salt and freshly ground pepper
Serves 8-10

Melt the butter in a large pan and fry the onions in it until soft. Add the potatoes and toss gently. Pour in the stock, wine and herbs and season with salt and freshly ground pepper. Cover with a lid and continue to cok over a medium heat for 10 minutes.

Transfer the entire mixture to a large shallow dish and bake in a preheated oven at 190°C/375°F/Gas Mark 5 for about 1 hour, until the potatoes are hot and the top is crisp.

PASTA, BRIE, CELERY AND WALNUT SALAD

500g/1lb fusilli, penne or similar pasta
250g/8oz Brie (or Camembert)
250g/8oz soft blue cheese, such as Gorgonzola
   or ripe Stilton
1/2 head of crisp celery, chopped
a handful of halved walnuts
6 tablespoons extra virgin olive oil
2 tablespoons fresh lemon juice
2 tablespoons walnut oil
salt and freshly ground pepper
radicchio leaves
fresh chopped parsley
Serves 4

Cook the pasta in boiling salted water until *al dente*. Then drain and rinse with cold water.

Cut the cheese into chunks and stir into the pasta with the remaining ingredients. Leave the salad for half an hour or so for the flavours to mix.

Serve in a bowl lined with radicchio leaves and scatter with chopped parsley.

RED SALAD

A large bowl of red salads looks festive while also satisfying those who yearn for something fresh and crisp with their Christmas food. Choose red leaves such as radicchio, red-tipped chicory, oak-leaf lettuce, lollo rosso and opal basil.

A nut-oil dressing would work well here: substitute two-thirds of the olive oil in your usual vinaigrette dressing for a walnut or hazelnut oil. Also scatter over a handful of chopped toasted walnuts if you wish.

STUFFED PANETTONE

1 Panettone
1lb tub Mascarpone cheese
125g/4oz chocolate chips or grated chocolate
grated rind of 1 large orange
125g/4fl oz cream, softly whipped
4 tablespoons brandy, sherry or rum or to taste
Serves 6-8

Slice the top from the Panettone. Scoop out most of the filling with a spoon to leave a Panettone 'shell' into which you will put the Mascarpone. Take care not to break the walls of the cake.

Break the filling into small crumbs and set aside. Mix the Mascarpone with the chocolate chips, whipped cream and the orange rind. Carefully stir in the alcohol and half of the cake crumbs (use the remaining ones for trifle or toasting and scattering over ice-creams).

Pile the filling back into the hollowed-out shell, replace the lid and dust with icing sugar. Chill for 25 minutes.

To serve: slice the Panettone horizontally into 3¾cm/1½inch thick slices, then cut each piece into quarters. Serve three or four pieces per person, dusted with a little icing sugar.

SAUTERNES JELLY

250g/8oz granulated sugar
250ml/½ pint water
1 pint water
300ml/10fl oz Sauternes (or a Muscat)
6 sheets/3 rounded teaspoons gelatine
Makes 4-6 small jellies

Boil the sugar and half the water rapidly for 5 minutes. Add the remaining water and the gelatine, and stir until dissolved. Leave to cool until tepid, then pour in the wine. Pour into glasses and leave in the refrigerator until just set. (*Note:* This is a fragile jelly and is not suitable for setting in a mould and turning out.)

HONEY-BAKED MINCEMEAT APPLES

4 large cooking apples
8 tablespoons vegetarian mincemeat
6 large dried apricots, chopped
50g/2oz walnuts, chopped
2 tablespoons brandy
6 tablespoons liquid honey
Serves 4

Core the apples and cut a fine line around the horizon of each apple. Place them in a baking dish in which they will sit snugly. Mix the mincemeat with the apricots and walnuts, then stuff the hollow apples with the mincemeat.

Stir the brandy and honey together, then spoon over the apples. Bake in a preheated oven at 200°C/400°F/Gas Mark 6 for about 45–50 minutes depending on their size. The apples are done when the fruit is fluffy.

MINCEMEAT

500g/1lb apples, peeled, cored and finely
* chopped or grated*
250g/8oz shredded suet (optional)
300g/10oz raisins
250g/8oz sultanas
250g/8oz currants
250g/8oz mixed peel
50g/2oz melted butter
300g/10oz soft brown sugar
3 teaspoons mixed spice
1 teaspoon ground cinnamon
juice and rind 1 orange
juice and rind 1 lemon
5 tablespoons brandy
Makes about 6 pounds

Mix all the ingredients together, stir well and pack into clean jars. Seal and store until required.

CARAMELIZED FRUITS

1kg/2lb assorted fruits, strawberries, orange
* segments, kumquats, black grapes*
750g/1½lb granulated sugar
250ml/8fl oz water
½ tablespoon liquid glucose
Makes 1kg/2lb of dipped fruits

Lightly oil a baking sheet with a flavourless oil such as groundnut. Put the sugar, water and glucose in a deep-sided pan and boil rapidly until the sugar has dissolved.

Cook the syrup until it starts to turn pale gold in colour, or reaches 143°C/290°F on a sugar thermometer. Remove from the heat and pour into a heatproof bowl sitting in a saucepan of hot water. Hold each piece of fruit by its stalk, or spear it with a skewer, then dip it into the caramel. Place each dipped fruit onto the oiled tray and leave to set. Eat them as soon as the coating is crisp and hard.

THE LATE, LATE CHRISTMAS PARTY

We used to have a large party every year on the Saturday before Christmas. However, eventually realizing that most people were either rather jaded around this time of year from having to go to so many business and private functions, or had gone away for the holiday, we decided to postpone the party to a drearier time of year – the third weekend in February – when it would be more appreciated.

For our annual Late, Late Christmas Party we decorate the house with greenery and flowers, much as over Christmas itself. Because between 120–180 people normally come I keep the food as simple as possible: a smoked mackerel pâté on toast and smoked salmon on brown bread, and all the hot savouries we serve on Christmas Eve (*see* pages 123–124). These are followed by a vegetarian lasagne and shepherd's pie with salad and, finally, "Eve's" apple and sponge pudding with custard. An Australian sparkling wine – such as Killawarra Rosé (approximately £4 a bottle) – makes a good accompaniment throughout the evening.

MUSIC & GAMES

As Christmas took over from the pagan festivals that preceded it (*see* pages 12–17), it also inherited their traditions of celebratory music and dance. The earliest carols, for example, took biblical stories of the birth of Christ as their theme and were arranged to popular tunes of their day. However, the medieval religious authorities disapproved of the "levity" of carols and so they were sung by the congregation outside the church after the festive service, where they were often accompanied by dancing. (The word 'carol' is derived from the French *caroler*, meaning to dance in a ring.)

By the 15th century, carol singing was permitted inside the church and the informal process of handing down tunes and lyrics by word of mouth from parents to children began to become more formalized. The first known collection of English carols was published in 1521, by Wynkyn de Worde (the original is kept in the Bodleian Library in Oxford).

Getting into the Christmas spirit with music and games was the order of the day by the 16th century, as Thomas Tusser noted in his *Five Hundred Points of Good Husbandry*, in 1580:

"At Christmas play, and make good cheer,
For Christmas comes but once a year."

However, for a brief period under Cromwell's rule in the middle of the 17th century carols were out in the cold once more, the Puritans considering them an inappropriate form of worship. These killjoys even abolished the Christmas festival altogether in 1647!

The restoration of the monarchy in 1660 saw the return of music, dance and drama to the theatres and public places. However, within the framework of the church service the folk tradition of carolling was not whole-heartedly rediscovered until the Victorian era.

In the 1850s one Reverend J.M. Neale unearthed a collection of 16th-century Swedish carols, *Piae Cantiones*. Neale translated many of them into English, including the famous "Good King Wenceslas", and published them as sheet music. Many other publishers followed suit, and a huge range of carols, old and new, became available to the music-loving Victorian public. Other popular carols of the time included "God Rest you Merry Gentlemen", "The Holly and the Ivy", "We Three Kings of Orient are" and "In the Bleak Midwinter", the words to the latter being penned by the poet, Christina Rossetti.

During the 19th century, carols didn't just find their way back into church. It became the custom on Christmas Eve for groups of singers to tour the streets belting them out at the tops of their voices, and to be invited into houses for a warming glass of punch and a plate of hot mince pies, a tradition that survives to this day. The Victorian carol singers were also known as "wassailers",

Right: *Martin and I welcome the carol-singers to Chilston with a traditional plate of mince pies – something a little stronger to fortify against the cold was available inside.*

after their pagan ancestors – bands of youths who roamed the fields around the time of New Year banging drums, clashing symbols and shouting at the top of their voices to ward off evil spirits (*see* pages 12–17).

For those who preferred more professional entertainment the Victorian pantomime, with its roots in *commedia dell'arte*, was the thing. From Boxing Day onward, families flocked to theatres up and down the land to see shows such as "Harlequin and Puss in Boots" or "Hey Diddle Diddle". Just like today's pantomimes, the 19th-century versions all featured a medley of popular tunes and scant attention, if any, was paid to the plot. The successful productions relied on lavish sets, huge casts, elaborate costumes and astonishing masks to attract the crowds.

Today, some people like to turn off the television and revive the Victorian custom of reciting poetry or singing songs around the piano in order to entertain the family and friends at Christmas. Our children, Tasha, Cara and Kirsty, usually take the opportunity to demonstrate the progress they've made in their school music lessons by playing seasonal tunes on the flute and recorder, accompanied by their nanny, Frances, on the piano.

Although the Victorian Mater and Pater would also take up the violin or turn to the piano at this time of year, Martin and I wouldn't dream of inflicting our shortcomings in this area on our family or guests, preferring to leave it to the professionals and the hi-fi. Perennial favourites include Bach's *Christmas Oratorio*, Handel's *Messiah*, Benjamin Britten's *St Nicholas Cantata* and his *Ceremony of the Carols*, and a "fun" piece by Leopold Mozart (Wolfgang's father) – *Musical Sleigh Ride in F major*, which includes special effects such as sleigh bells, the crack of the driver's whip and cheers from the sleighing party. *Santa Claus is Coming to Town* by Bruce Springsteen has also been known to resound around the house – at the request, of course, of the children.

If there was one thing that the Victorians loved at Christmas as much as music, it was games. 19th-century celebrations were considered incomplete without them. One of the most popular was "Snapdragon" – a fearsome affair centred around a dish filled with spirit and placed on the floor. The spirit was ignited and handfuls of currants were thrown in; the aim of the game being to snatch a burning currant out of the flame in your mouth and in so doing extinguish it!

In today's litigious times we would advise against reintroducing this particular game at children's Christmas

Right: *Accompanied by their nanny, Frances, on the piano, Tasha (left), Cara (middle) and Kirsty (right) give a festive recital for family and friends gathered at Chilston. Gathering round the piano to sing carols and songs was an essential part of the Christmas celebrations in many Victorian and Edwardian households – a tradition that has largely, and sadly, fallen into general decline since the advent of television during the second half of the 20th century.*

Left: *"Glad tidings" by William M. Spittle (1858-1917). Carol singers ("wassailers"), accompanied by a cellist and oboe player, bring glad tidings of joy to the squire of the local manor.*

parties. However, there are plenty of other traditional games that don't carry a safety warning – for example, "Blind Man's Buff", "Hide-and-Seek", "Bob Apple", "Hunt the Slipper" and "Charades" were all Victorian favourites that have survived to this day. (Others that have fallen by the wayside included "Spinning the Trencher", "Hot Cockles", "Puss in the Corner" and "Steal the White Loaf".)

"Blind Man's Buff" was known to have been played at Christmas as early as the 16th century, and was originally

fire risk – the apples bobbing on the surface of a pail of water. With hands behind their backs, each player attempts to pick up an apple in his or her mouth. The first to succeed is the winner.

In "Hunt the Slipper" one player is picked out once more, this time to sit in the middle of a circle of revellers. The slipper is passed around the circle, behind the backs of the players, while music is played. When the music is stopped, the player in the middle has to guess which player is in possession of the slipper.

known as "Hoodman-Blind". The game involves one player being blindfolded with a scarf and then spun around three times. The task is then to try and catch another player and guess the identity of the captive. If the guess is correct, the captive takes on the blindfold, but if incorrect the blindfold is endured until another player has been caught and correctly identified.

"Hide-and-seek" involves one player hunting down the others, who have hidden themselves in nooks and cupboards, under beds and behind doors around the house.

"Bob-apple" is rather like "Snapdragon" without the

"Spinning the Trencher" involved appropriating a wooden breadboard from the kitchen. One player stands in the middle of the room and twirls the trencher while calling out the name of another of the players in the room. This player has to move fast to catch the trencher before it falls. If he or she fails, a forfeit has to be paid.

Another good game is "Passing the Matchbox". The players form sides and kneel on the floor facing each other about a yard apart – and with their arms folded behind their backs. The outer case of a matchbox is then placed at the end of each row, in front of the first player, who has to pick it up with his nose and pass it on to the next player's nose . . . and so on until the end of the row, and back again. If the box is dropped it must be picked up by the nose by the player who dropped it. The side which finishes first wins.

"Dusting Chairs" is another favourite. The players divide into two sides – girls on one and boys on the other. The girls go out of the room, while the boys each stand behind an empty chair and choose one of the girls. The girls then come in one at a time, and sit in front of the

boy who she thinks is most likely to have chosen her. If correct, he kisses her, but if not she is hissed out of the room and the next player enters.

"Charades", also popular since Victorian times, involves dividing the assembled company into two teams. One side then secretly chooses a word of two, three or more syllables, and a representative to act it out silently syllable by syllable. The other side then has to guess what the word is, within a set time limit. (Many families in Victorian times and the early years of the 20th century kept a "dress-up box" of discarded, outmoded clothes that

were used to add to the enjoyment of the charade.)

For quieter tastes or smaller family gatherings, traditional board games were favoured. Today, our children enjoy playing tiddlywinks, dominoes, draughts and chess, especially with our period counters and pieces, while we, during the quieter moments, always try to get in a few hands of bridge.

Of course, we do watch television at Christmas. Although this can hardly be described as traditional entertainment, the Victorian did in fact enjoy a pre-

cursor to the ubiquitous box – the Magic Lantern. This was an early projector, with hand-painted coloured slides depicting such delights as famous actresses, animals, boats and familiar architecture and landscapes.

Because the Magic Lantern was such a novel piece of equipment, it was only brought out to entertain guests on special occasions. In much the same way, Martin and I try to restrict the use of the television over Christmas – with so many entertaining games to play it's one time of the year when there really is no excuse to lapse into being a couch potato.

COUNTDOWN TO CHRISTMAS

Our Countdown to Christmas is intended to take the stress out of buying and preparing food for the festival.

It is designed around the suggested recipes for Christmas Eve supper, Christmas Day breakfast, lunch and high tea, and Boxing Day breakfast and buffet, given on pages 123–146, and also incorporates suggested times for making edible presents (*see pages 82–83*).

Many of the specific times for the preparation of various dishes are given on the assumption that other members of the family are available to help out in the kitchen.

By following the Countdown you should avoid any last-minute panics and consequently have more time to relax and enjoy yourself with family and friends.

EARLY NOVEMBER

Make Christmas puddings (*page 134*).

MID-NOVEMBER

Make mincemeat (*page 146*).
Make Christmas cake (*pages 138–139*).
Contact mail-order suppliers (*pages 157–158*) to order free-range poultry, meat and Christmas hampers.

BEGINNING OF DECEMBER

Almond paste the Christmas cake.
Order poultry and meat from butcher.
Order wine.

10TH–15TH DECEMBER

Ice Christmas cake (*page 139*).
Make herb oils and flower vinegars (*pages 82–83*).
Make and freeze puff pastry straws (*page 124*), Marmite pinwheels (*page 124*), spicy sausage rolls (*page 123*), anchovy palmiers (*page 142*) and vegetarian rolls (*page 123*).
Make and freeze mince pies (*page 126*).
Make and freeze stocks for two soups (*pages 124 and 130*).
Make gilded gingerbread (*page 83*), wrap in foil and store in air-tight container.

16TH–20TH DECEMBER

Order vegetables from greengrocer.
Make caramelized fruits (*page 146*)
Make Christmas cookies (*page 65*) and store in an air-tight container.
Make fruit bread (*page 136*), wrap in tin foil and store in air-tight container.
Make shortbread (*page 139*) and store in air-tight container.

23RD DECEMBER

Thaw frozen turkey or goose in a cool room (not in the refrigerator).
Make brandy butter (*page 136*).
Make Cumberland sauce (*page 134*) and refrigerate.
Make Christmas pudding ice-cream (*page 136*) and freeze.
Make turkey and chestnut pie (*page 142*).

CHRISTMAS EVE (MORNING)

Prepare apricots and prunes in bacon (*page 125*) and refrigerate.
Make stuffings for poultry (*pages 130 and 132*) and refrigerate.
Make chestnut roast (*page 132*) and refrigerate.
Prepare fish pie (*page 125*) and refrigerate.
Prepare stocks for gravies (*page 130 and 132*).

CHRISTMAS EVE (AFTERNOON)

Make fruits dipped in chocolate (*page 83*).

CHRISTMAS EVE (EVENING)

(Guests arriving around 8.00pm for supper at 9.00pm)
5.00pm: Put white wine in fridge.
6.00pm: Prepare peas, bacon and baby onions (*page 125*).
Remove mince pies from freezer and bake in hot oven.
Make vegetable consommé (*page 124*).
Peel potatoes for Christmas Day breakfast.
7.30pm: Prepare mulled wine (*page 123*).
Remove puff pastry nibbles from freezer and put straight into a hot oven.
8.00pm: Open red wine.
8.15pm: Put fish pie into hot oven.
8.30pm: Cook peas, bacon and baby onions.
8.45pm: Heat vegetable consommé.
11.15pm: Make egg nog (*page 125*).
12.30am: Put mince pies into hot oven (*page 126*). Put champagne in fridge for following morning.

CHRISTMAS DAY

(Breakfast between 9.00am–10.00am, lunch at 1.30pm and high tea at 7.00pm. The times given for the preparation of various dishes for lunch – such as gilding the Christmas pudding – are fairly flexible, and assume that the entire meal is a leisurely affair that takes place over anything between two to three hours.)
8.00am: Stuff the turkey or goose (*pages 130–132*).
8.30am: Put bird in preheated oven.

9.00am: Make stuffed papaya (*page 126*), potato pancakes (*page 126*) and marmalade muffins (*page 126*) for breakfast.
10.30am: Peel potatoes and prepare sprouts (*page 132*).
Steam Christmas pudding (*page 134*).
11.00am: Make Stilton soup (*page 130*).
Put white wine in fridge.
11.30am: Prepare garnishes for poultry (*pages 130–132*).
Prepare honey-baked apples.
12.00am: Bring potatoes to boil for 5 minutes, drain, then place in oven with bird.
12.30am: Put chestnut roast and sweet potatoes in oven.
Turn up oven and remove foil to brown turkey or goose.
1.00pm: Grill sausages and bacon rolls (*pages 130–132*).
Open red wine.
1.15pm: Remove bird from oven, make gravy and heat Cumberland sauce.
Remove vegetable parcels (*page 133*) from freezer and put into hot oven.
1.25pm: Cook sprouts and chestnuts.
1.50pm: Remove Christmas pudding from heat and leave to cool for half an hour, prior to gilding.
2.20pm: Gild Christmas pudding.
Remove Christmas pudding ice-cream from freezer (just before serving).
5.00pm: Delegate washing-up.
6.00pm: Prepare Stilton rarebit and Kitchen Garden salad (*page 136*).
8.30pm: Poach fruits for Boxing Day breakfast (*page 140*). Make Sauternes jellies (*page 146*) and refrigerate.

BOXING DAY

(Breakfast around 9.30am and guests arrive at midday for lunchtime buffet at 1.30pm.)
8.30am: Make kedgeree (*page 140*).
10.00am: Prepare stuffed Panettone (*page 143*).
10.30am: Prepare pasta, Brie and walnut salad (*page 143*).
Prepare red salad (*page 143*).
Put white wine in fridge.
11.00am: Prepare boulangère potatoes (*page 143*).
12.00am: Remove anchovy palmiers from freezer and place in hot oven.
Make fruit punch.
Remove turkey and chestnut pie from fridge.
Prepare caramelized fruits.
1.30pm: Open red wine.

BOXES

Panduro Hobby
FREEPOST
Westway House
Transport Avenue
Brentford
Middx TW8 8BR
Tel: 081-847-6161
Suppliers of birch boxes. Extensive mail order catalogue available. Minimum order £22.50.

The Secret Garden
153 Regent Street
London W1
Tel: 071-439-3107
Papier mâché boxes

The Shaker Shop
25 Harcourt Street
London W1
071-724-7672
Shaker-style wooden boxes (plain and painted) available. Also gift boxes, hampers and baskets.

CAKE DECORATIONS

Cake Decor
6 The Arcade
Worthing
West Sussex
Tel: 0903-239215

Squires Kitchen
Sugarcraft
Squires House
3 Waverly Lane
Farnham
Surrey GU9 8BB
Tel: 0252-711749
Everything for decorating cakes – from food colours to cutters. Also, base boards, ribbons, decorating books, boxes and wrappings.

CANDLES

Candle Makers Supplies
28 Blythe Road
London W14
Tel: 071-602-4031

Prices Candles
110 York Road
London SW11
Tel: 071-228-3345
Suppliers of candles (all colours) and angel chimes to shops and wholesalers.

Shimmers Beeswax Candles
60 Wood End Road
Kempston
Bedford
Bedfordshire
Tel: 0234-856639
Beeswax candles in traditional honey colours, plus scarlet, pine, ivory and pastel shades.

The Candle Shop
30 The Market
Covent Garden
London WC2
Tel: 071-836-9815
Vast range of candles, including Advent, custom-made red and green and small candles with tree clips.

CHEESE

Abergavenny Fine Foods Ltd
Pant-ys-gawn Farm
Mamhilad
Nr Pontypool
Gwent NP4 8RG
Tel: 0873-880844
Selection of Welsh cheeses available by post with a greetings card.

CHRISTMAS CARDS

The Winslow Papers
Hofman Trading Company
89 Barnhill
Wembley Park
Middx HA9 9LA
Tel: 081-904-4716
Suppliers to shops of wide range of greetings cards, tags and enclosures (all with Victorian theme).

CHRISTMAS PUDDINGS AND CAKES

Bettys-by-Post
1 Parliament Street
Harrogate
North Yorkshire HG1 2QU
Tel: 0423-531211
Mail order Christmas cakes, sent in seasonal tins.

Jacqui Holmes
Horn End Cottages
Low Mill
Farndale
Kirkbymoorside
Yorkshire YO6 6XA
Tel: 0751-33268 (after 8pm)
Traditional cakes and puddings, and gingerbread houses to commission.

Mosimann's
PHS Mailing Ltd
PO Box 14
Horley
Surrey RH6 8DW
Tel: 0293-77208
Suppliers of Christmas puddings.

Queen of Hearts Bakery
Sandy Lane West
Littlemore
Oxford OX4 5JS
Tel: 0865-718080
Puddings and cakes, made from the finest natural ingredients, posted direct.

The Village Bakery
Melmerby
Penrith
Cumbria CA10 1HE
Tel: 0768-81515
Selection of Christmas cakes and puddings made from organic ingredients. (Some are suitable for vegans.)

CONFECTIONERY

Clarkes of Loch Ewe
Home Place
Coldstream
Berwickshire TD12 4DT
Tel: 0890-3153
Hand-made chocolates by post.

Humphreys Exclusive Confectionery
16 Leeds Road
Ilkley LS29 8DJ
Tel: 0943-609477
Christmas pudding-shaped chocolates by post.

Kinnells
36 Victoria Street
Edinburgh EH1 2JP
Tel: 031-220-1150
Mail order hand-made chocolates and chocolate-coated beans.

Thorntons
Thornton Park
Somercotes
Derby DE55 4XJ
Tel: 0773-608822 for stockists
Makers of a wide range of gift-wrapped chocolates. Also chocolate Christmas pudding- and cake-shaped truffles.

CRACKERS

Grey Goose Crackers
Mariskall House
Mill Road
Felsted
Great Dunmow
Essex
Tel: 0371-820315
Handmade crackers in three sizes, and containing useful gifts such as picture frames, torches and pens, available via department stores and gift shops.

Present Surprise
161-165 Greenwich High Road
London SE10 8JA
Tel: 081-293-4335
Luxury crackers at varying prices according to contents. "Next day" delivery service available.

Tom Smith Crackers
Sarhouse Road
Norwich
Norfolk NR7 9AS
Tel: 0603-404904
Suppliers to wholesalers of a wide range of crackers containing traditional hats, snaps and small gifts.

Upper Crust Crackers
The Old Barn
Hall Farm
Bentworth
Alton
Hants GU34 3TD
Tel: 0420-62459
Exclusive range of hand-made crackers, containing useful gifts such as Nottingham lace coasters, rosewood fruit knives and penknives. A brochure is available.

DRIED FLOWERS AND POT-POURRI

Angela Flanders
The Flower Room
94-96 Columbia Road
London E2 7QB
Tel: 071-739-7555
Pot-pourri, room sprays and burning oil, as well as aromatic and fragrant essences.

Chattels
53 Chalk Farm Road
London NW1
Tel: 071-267-0877
Specialists in dried flowers, pot-pourri and basketware. Wreaths and seasonal table arrangements available.

Heaven Scent
Square Bookhams Cottage
Nursery
Dunsford
Nr Exeter EX6 7DL
Tel: 0647-24544
Garlands and swags of dried flowers.

Paula Pryke Flowers
20 Penton Street
London N1 9PS
Tel: 071-837-7336
Fresh and dried flower arrangements to order. Also pot-pourri. Houses and offices decorated for Christmas.

Verandah
156 Blenheim Crescent
London W11 2EE
Tel: 071-792-9289
Pomanders and mixtures of cinnamon sticks, cloves and cones available.

FLAVOURED OILS AND VINEGARS

The Fresh Food Company
100 Bayswater Road
London W2 3HJ
Tel: 071-402-5414
Mail order only.

GENERAL

Anta
141 Portland Road
London W11
Tel: 071-229-5077
Tartan throws, rugs, cushions and ceramics available.

Celia Birtwell
71 Westbourne Park Road
London W2
Tel: 071-221-0877
A wide range of materials for decorating the house – gold stars a speciality.

Hankin and Co.
St Margaret
Harleston
Norfolk IP20 0PJ
Tel: 0986-82536
Extensive selection of Victorian scraps, paper chains etc. Mail order.

Liberty
Regent Street
London W1
Tel: 071-734-1234
Liberty's distinctive fabric designs provide many gift ideas – large and small. Near to Christmas a special department is open selling decorations and a wide range of wrappings and ribbons.

Lunn Antiques
86 New King's Road
London SW6
Tel: 071-736-4638
Antique presents and lace accessories, including lavender bags and cushions.

Penhaligons
41 Wellington Street
London WC2
Tel: 071-606-5355
A wide range of attractively packaged toiletries available, including cracker-wrapped perfume bottles and hat boxes filled with gift selections.

Selfridges
Oxford Street
London W1
Tel: 071-629-1234
In-store Christmas Hall sells all kinds of decorations, trees, papers and gifts.

The Conran Shop
81 Fulham Road
London SW3 6RD
Tel: 071-589-7401
A wide selection of candles, gifts, tree decorations, ribbons, papers, fabric stockings and special food and chocolates available.

The Dining Room Shop
68 White Hart Lane
London SW13
Tel: 081-878-1020
A wide range of table accessories, including china and glass – mostly antique – and linens and candles available.

The General Trading Company
144 Sloane Street
London W1
Tel: 071-730-0411
Suppliers of a wide range of small presents, decorations and Christmas stationery.

"Un jardin . . . en plus" Great Britain
100 Mount Street
Mayfair
London W1
Tel: 071-528-4444
Suppliers of many items including serviettes, candlesticks, tree decorations and boxes.

HAMPERS AND GIFT BASKETS

Apples by the Box
Charlton Orchards
Creech St Michael
Taunton
Somerset TA3 5PF
Tel: 0823-412979
Mail order only.

Basket Express
4 Vale Close
Maida Vale
London W9 1RR
Tel: 071-289-2636
Selections of nuts, glacé and dried fruits in decorative baskets.

Elizabeth the Chef
Mail Order Division
Unit 1
5 Beaconsfield St West
Leamington Spa
Warwickshire CV33 1DH
Tel: 0926-885114
Supply a wide range of hampers, puddings and hand-made cakes.

Fortnum and Mason
181 Piccadilly
London W1A 1ER
Tel: 071-734-8040
Hampers available in a wide range of sizes and price tags. With fresh or non-perishable contents, including a selection of tea, coffee and relishes to customers' orders.

Harrods
87-135 Brompton Road
Knightsbridge
London SW1X 7XL
Tel: 071-589-1490
Hampers made up to customers' orders from a wide range of products from their elegant, world famous Food Halls. Ideal for last minute Christmas shopping.

Taylors of Oxford
31 St Giles
Oxford OX1 3LD
Tel: 0865-58853
Range of hampers and gift baskets, packed to order and shipped worldwide. Includes own-brand chocolates and wine, and a wide variety of biscuits and pâtés.

Telefruit
202-204 Long Lane
London SE1 4QB
Tel: 071-403-0555
Gift baskets of food delivered nationwide to order.

The Highland Connection
Earsdon Hill
Morpeth
Northumberland NE61 3ES
Write for details.
Gamekeeper hampers supplied.

Unirose Gift Service
Mount Ephrain Farm
Cranbrook
Kent
Tel: 0580-714011
Selection of hampers containing champagne, caviare and smoked salmon. Also selection of drink in wooden crates. Brochure available.

FRUITS IN LIQUEUR

Trustin Foods
Chase Road
Northern Way
Bury St Edmonds
Suffolk IP32 6NT
Tel: 0284-766265
Suppliers of Dartington Foods, who produce a range of liqueured fruits, such as pineapples in kirsch, summer fruits in Muscat wine and mandarins in orange liqueur.

POULTRY AND MEAT

Church Farm
Strixton
Wellingborough
Northants NN9 7PA
Tel: 0933-664378
Suppliers of Norfolk Blacks – a variety of the Cambridge Bronze turkey renowned for its rich, gamey flavour.

Dukeshill Ham Company
Bridgenorth
Shropshire WV16 6AF
Tel: 074-635-519
Mail order only for traditional cooked and uncooked hams.

R&J Lodge
"Pies and Cheese" Courier Service
Greens End Road
Meltham
Huddersfield HD7 3NW
Tel: 0484-850571
Mail order service for traditional pork and game pies (and cheese). Brochure available.

Real Meat Direct
East Hill Farm
Heytesbury
Nr Warminster
Wiltshire BA12 0HR
Tel: 0985-40436
Suppliers of poultry and meat (raised in humane free-range conditions).

Sir Julian Rose
Hardwick Estate Office
Whitchurch
Reading RG8 7RB
Tel: 0734-842955
Suppliers of organically raised turkeys approved by the Soil Association.

The Pure Meat Company
Moretonhampstead
Devon TQ13 8QP
Tel: 0647-40321
Supliers of poultry and meat raised in humane free-range conditions.

Traditional Farmfresh Turkey Association
5 Beacon Drive
Seaford
East Sussex BN25 2JX
Tel: 0323-899802
Contact to find your local suppliers.

Wholefood Butchers
31 Paddington Street
London W1M 4DR
Tel: 071-486-1390
Organic and free-range turkeys available. Also chicken, ducks and other poultry.

PRESERVES

Crabtree and Evelyn London Ltd
36 Milton Park
Abingdon
Oxon OX14 4RT
Tel: 0235-864824
Suppliers of preserves, tea and chocolates in attractively packaged tins. Available nationwide.

Culpepper Ltd
Hadstock Road
Linton
Cambridge CB1 6NJ
Tel: 0223-894054
Suppliers of an extensive range of preserves and herbs.

The National Trust
Tel: 0225 705676 for catalogue
Attractively wrapped preserves (and biscuits).

SMOKED SALMON

Benester Shellfish Farm and Orkney Smokehouse
Old School House
Deerness
Orkney KW17 2QH
Tel: 085-674-267
Suppliers of smoked and whisky-smoked salmon. Also smoked scallops, oysters and mussels, marinaded herrings, smoked salmon sausage and pastiche, smoked Orkney cheese. Mail order only. Hampers available.

Inverawe Smokehouses
Taynuilt
Argyll
Tel: 086-62-446
Smoked salmon by post.

Otter Ferry Salmon Ltd
Otter Ferry
Tighnabruaich
Argyll PA2 2DH
Tel: 070-082-267
Smoked salmon by post.

STENCILS

The Quiltery
Newey Mill
Tipton D74 8AH
Tel: 021-522-2500
Stainless steel stencils with Christmas designs and an extensive range of paints and brushes available.

The Stencil Store
91 Lower Sloane Street
London SW1
Tel: 071-730-0728
Stencils with a Christmas theme – santas, reindeer and holly etc. – and paints and brushes available.

STORAGE JARS AND TINS

Divertimenti
45-47 Wigmore Street
London W1
Tel: 071-935-0689
139 Fulham Road
London SW3
Tel: 071-581-8065
All shapes and sizes of cake tins sold, including round and hexagonal. Also Christmas tree and Santa pans, glass jars for storage and preserving, and stainless steel tins for sugar and dried goods.

Lakeland Plastics Ltd
Alexandra Buildings
Windermere
Cumbria LA23 1BQ
Tel: 05394-88100
Christmas catalogue available from September.

TREE DECORATIONS

Gisela Graham
12 Colworth Grove
Browning Street
London SE17 1LR
Tel: 071-708-4956
Exclusive designs available, including baubles. Also snow domes and gift boxes.

Heals
196 Tottenham Court Road
London W1
Tel: 071-636-1666
Large selection of decorations – lights and baubles to garlands and chains.

Konstmide
Yew Tree Farm
Hardstoft
Chesterfield S45 8AE
Tel: 0246-852140
Christmas tree lights via mail order.

Neal Street East
5 Neal Street
London WC2 9PU
Tel: 071-240-0135
Clip-on candle holders and small decorations such as wooden chairs, straw hats and baskets available.

Paper Safari
379 Upper Richmond Road West
London SW14 7NX
Tel: 081-876-5631
A wide range of decorations, including ribbons, swags and garlands, available. (Also mail order.)

Saint Nicolas
26 Wingate Road
London W6
Tel: 081-749-6384
Hand-made felt decorations embellished with braids, beads and sequins.

Tobias and the Angel
68 White Hart Lane
London SW13
Tel: 081-878-8902
Glass and papier mâché baubles a speciality. Also cones, wreaths, gilded pots and small candles.

TREES

Quinto International
26 Warren Road
Guildford GU1 2HB
Tel: 0428-714123
Mail order only for traditional red and green wooden tree tubs.

The British Christmas Tree Association
12 Lauriston Road
London SW19 4TQ
Tel: 081-946-2695
Contact for information on buying and caring for trees.

The Chelsea Gardener
125 Sydney Street
London SW3 6NR
Tel: 071-352-5656
Norway spruce, blue spruce and Scots pine available, plus decorations.

TRADITIONAL PRESENTS

Adele Welsby Samplers
Sandbanks
Beaumaris
Anglesey
Gwynedd LL58 8YX
Tel: 0248-811355
Choice of four traditional decorative sampler designs for cross-stitch embroidery available in presentation packs.

Malvern Kites
St Annes Road
Malvern WR14 4PZ
Tel: 06845-65504
Stock a wide range of kites, from the simple to the exotic, and in numerous colours and designs.

Mary Hansen
PO Box 869
London SW11 4HU
Tel: 071-622-8838
Stock traditional cross-stitch kits from The Danish Handicraft Guild. Catalogue available.

Penfriend
Bush House Arcade
Bush House
Strand
London WC2
Tel: 071-836-9809
Stockists of a wide range of new and vintage pens, also antique writing implements, including quills and Victorian inkwells.

Thomas Goode
19 South Audley Street
London W1
Tel: 071-499-2823
Antique presents – from stud boxes to cushions – and a wide selection of tableware and glass in traditional and modern designs available (also via catalogue).

WRAPPINGS AND PACKING, PAPER AND RIBBONS

Brighteyes
8 Wynyatt Street
London EC1V 7HU
Tel: 071-833-1541
Suppliers of paper gift wrappings to retail outlets.

Falkiner Fine Papers
76 Southampton Row
London WC1B 4AR
Tel: 071-831-1151
Wide selection of hand-made papers available, including varieties made from, for example, bracken, wool and flax.

Paperchase
213 Tottenham Court Road
London W1P 9AF
Tel: 071-580-8496
Carry a large stock of Christmas decorations for the house and tree, plus gift wrappings and cards.

Specialist Crafts
PO Box 247
Leicestershire LE1 9QS
Tel: 0533-510405
A range of papers and coloured card available via mail order catalogue.

V V Rouleaux
201 Kings Road
London SW6 4SR
Tel: 071-371-5929
Specialize exclusively in ribbons – a vast range available, including wire-edged, silk, organza, checks, tartans, paper and antique, and virtually all the ribbons shown throughout the book.

INDEX

PICTURE CREDITS
The Bridgeman Art Library, London: 14TL (A & F Pears Ltd), 15BR (by courtesy of the Board of the Trustees of the V & A), 16TL (Private Collection), 17BL (Christie's), 36TC (Worthing Museum and Art Gallery, Sussex), 61 (Hirsch Sprungske Collection). **Mary Evans Picture Library, London:** 15TL (Cecil Aldin), 17CR (Godefroy Durand, Illustrated London News), 36BC, 74BR (HJ Schneider/Harriet Myrtle *Little Sister*), 75CL (*When Mother was a Little Girl*), 121CL/C/CR. By Courtesy of **Fine Art Photographic Library:** 4TL, 10-11, 13, 14BR, 16BR, 17TL, 74TL, 75BR, 152.

Index compiled by
Vicki Robinson
Directory compiled by
Frances Page

ACKNOWLEDGEMENTS

Creating this book involved the help and co-operation of a great number of people. The Publishers and Authors would especially like to thank: Saira Joshi at Thomas Goode for providing such wonderful crockery, Angela Flanders at The Flower Room for giving us so many traditional pot-pourris, Angel at Tobias and The Angel for lending the antique Christmas decorations, V.V. Rouleaux for supplying gorgeous ribbons (many antique), Amanda Wakeley for lending some of her exquisite designs, Tim at Hari's for hairstyling, Shane McMechan for advice on pop-up cards, Natalie Harris for advice on quillwork and gilding Christmas puddings, Hanse Schneider for all her work on location. Also Frances Page, Deborah Greatrex and the staff at Chilston Park Hotel, Lenham, Kent for feeding the crew. Others who helped produce this book are mentioned on the copyright page but a special note of thanks is due to Jeremy Roots.